Also by Titus Joseph

Our Curious World of Mirror Images:
Reflections on how Symmetry Frames our Universe
Empowers the Creative Process,
and Provides Context to Shape our Lives

I AM 'MIND,' I AM 'CONSCIOUSNESS'

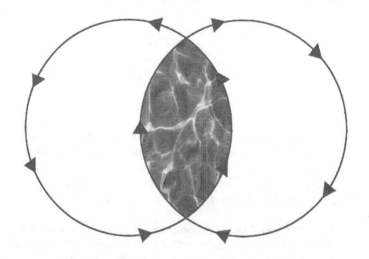

How To Come Back To The Remembrance Of God Through *Cosmosis*

Titus Joseph

BALBOA
PRESS

A DIVISION OF HAY HOUSE

Balboa Press books may be ordered through booksellers or by contacting:

Balboa Press
A Division of Hay House
1663 Liberty Drive
Bloomington, IN 47403
www.balboapress.com
1 (877) 407-4847

Because of the dynamic nature of the Internet, any web addresses or links contained in this book may have changed since publication and may no longer be valid. The views expressed in this work are solely those of the author and do not necessarily reflect the views of the publisher, and the publisher hereby disclaims any responsibility for them.

The author of this book does not dispense medical advice or prescribe the use of any technique as a form of treatment for physical, emotional, or medical problems without the advice of a physician, either directly or indirectly. The intent of the author is only to offer information of a general nature to help you in your quest for emotional and spiritual well-being. In the event you use any of the information in this book for yourself, which is your constitutional right, the author and the publisher assume no responsibility for your actions.

Any people depicted in stock imagery provided by Thinkstock are models, and such images are being used for illustrative purposes only. Certain stock imagery © Thinkstock.

Print information available on the last page.

ISBN: 978-1-5043-5668-8 (sc)
ISBN: 978-1-5043-5670-1 (hc)
ISBN: 978-1-5043-5669-5 (e)

Library of Congress Control Number: 2016906931

Balboa Press rev. date: 09/29/2016

Contents

*How To Come Back
To The Remembrance Of God
Through Cosmosis*

"...the time cometh, when I shall
no more speak onto you in proverbs,
but I shall shew you plainly
of the *FATHER*."
John 16:25

"And the *FATHER* himself...
Ye have neither heard his voice at any time,
nor seen his shape."
John 5:37

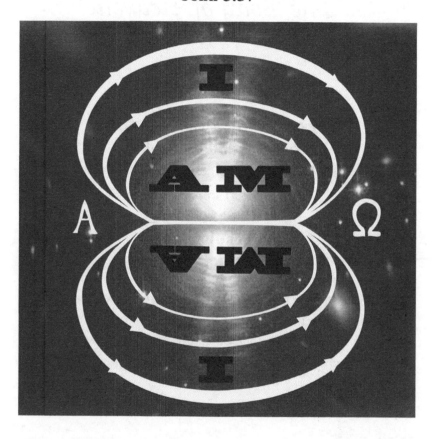

The Egg Nebulae   Hubble/NASA

"And they saw the **God** of **Israel:**
and there was under his feet as it were
a paved work of sapphire stone, and as it were
the *body of heaven in his clearness.*"
Exodus 24:10

The Cosmic Circuit:
The Body of Heaven

**"I AM ALPHA & OMEGA: The
Beginning and the Ending,**
saith the Lord, which is, and which was,
and *which is to come,*
The Almighty."
Revelation 1:8

What is the meaning of the phrase, Alpha and Omega, the Beginning and the End? What is the nature of the 'and,' or the reality that fills the gap from Beginning to the End? Is there anything in our reality that we can refer to when we think of the meaning in the expression, Alpha and Omega?

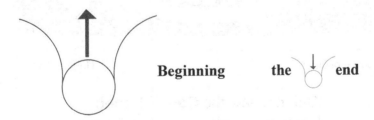

Beginning   **the**   **end**

Clue: The flow of events (stories)…over time…

"The lord is the portion of mine
inheritance and of my cup:
thou maintainest my lot.
The lines are fallen unto me in pleasant places;
yea I have a goodly heritage.
I will bless the Lord who hath given me counsel;
my reins also instruct me in the night seasons."
Psalm 16:5-7

For Example:

"It is he that buildeth his stories [history?]
in the heaven,
...*He that calleth for the waters of the sea,*
and poureth them upon the face of the earth:"
Amos 9:6

Answer: The "space" between the beginning and the end, is a thing we call, 'spacetime.'

"Do not I fill heaven and earth? Saith the Lord."
Jeremiah 23:24

The appearance of any object as an "existing thing" implies an active and ongoing process of *being*. We are all very much acquainted with this principle in life's ordinary experiences. The child, for example, comes into being at the beginning, undergoing developmental changes, in stages. Time is implicit in this process and indeed, in any process. With the abundance of knowledge that we have of reality today, one must come to understand intuitively that so is space.

Time and space extends beyond the immediate here and now, it expands to form the immaterial body of the *Cosmos;* which in itself, is its own being, and I think that it is reasonable to say that the Cosmos is very likely the ultimate Being.

The Cosmos serves as the context, the backdrop, the past—from which existing things materialize into being. When we use the instruments of science to peer through space and time, the spacetime that we see is literally of the *past*, because, the light that arrives here now, had started its journey a long, long time ago. When we look through space and time, *we only see the past*. This means in a practical sense that most of the universe that is present now, is invisible to us whose consciousness is embedded and limited to the here and now.

The universe, to the extent that it provides context for all things, accordingly, it must serve as the template for all things. All things, it is reasonable to assume, are made in its image. Even so, the cosmos may be as a fruit on the Tree's branch. Our scientists speak of the multiverse but I will speak of the metaverse.

Remember the ancient stories of the Hebrews. There are written documents in the accounts of the Hebrews in which the God of Israel is manifested, plainly, for us to see. The book of Exodus, for example, provides us with an intriguing narrative.

According to Exodus 24:1-11; Moses, Aaron, Nadab, Abihu, and seventy of the elders of Israel, saw the God of Israel. The story relays a scenario of a Supreme Being *standing in space and time.* This 'Being,' according to the tradition, appears to be the person of God, and who is this God? Curiously, the God of Israel is described, in-part, as, *"the body of heaven in his clearness."*

The body of heaven, or, the Cosmos, is filled with clear, transparent, immaterial, translucent, space and time. Space fills the expanse from the beginning to the end, and time bridges the void. Though it is not necessarily intuitive, we now know today through Einstein's beautiful inspiration, that space and time exist as one entity called spacetime. Spacetime exist in an inseparable ratio relationship that can be described as space divided by time. For more about the science and the metaphysics concerning the meaning in Alpha and Omega, read my first book, *Our Curious World Of Mirror Images: Reflections on how Symmetry Frames the Universe, Empowers the Creative Process, and Provides Context to Shape Our Lives.* This book develops a well-defined argument using science and philosophy to explain our world in spiritual terms naturally.

Spacetime has remarkable relativistic properties; it is extraordinarily slippery, so much so that you can have a lot of space in little time, or a lot of time in any given space. What I find particularly intriguing about the ancient Hebrew text is in that it refers to what is ostensibly, spacetime; using the pronoun, 'his,' i.e., "the body of heaven in his clearness."

Some of the attributes of God that we intuitively accept include ideas that God is everywhere (omni-present), all-knowing (omniscient), invisible, and all-powerful (omnipotent).

Given these attributes, lets start with something that we can quickly understand. What do we know of in our collective human experiences, that is literally everywhere? Well, spacetime is everywhere there is a where.

We typically think of spacetime as being four dimensions of length, width, height, and time. In fact, in the science of cosmology, there is another dimension called the *elsewhere.*[1] The elsewhere is spacetime that is so far away that the light from events from such distant places, have not reached us yet

---

[1] Wolfson, R., *Einstein's Relativity and the Quantum Revolution.* Parts 1-2, 2000, p147

4

in the here and now. The effect of this is as though there is a huge visible wave in the ocean of spacetime, a wall of light approaching us that we can see but it obscures anything behind it, and what is most interesting and compelling is that there is *no information* whatsoever that is accessible to us from the elsewhere. As a consequence, the elsewhere is a dimension of spacetime that cannot be considered to be of the past, nor future, it is 'elsewhere.' The elsewhere, is defined by its distance from the here and now, and fact that the speed of light has a limit.

The physics means that if we used a telescope to see the events of some distant space, what we would witness now, would be of what had transpired there *in the past*. The events that are occurring now, over there, are unknown, and thus cannot yet be considered a part of our time-line. If we think of the elsewhere as space beyond distant space, then the cousin of the 'elsewhere' in the dimension of time, is called the *"belt of non-causal time."*

Now we have become aware that there are dimensions of spacetime so far beyond the here and now that events that occur now over there, are not just unknown to us, but, by virtue of the laws of physics, since the light has not reached us yet, there can be no causal relations to the here and now.

No information from such distant places is accessible to us and as a consequence, no event occurring now over there, can affect us in any way in the here and now; even to the extent that we cannot even perceive it along the timeline. What this implies is that overall, there is a lot of space and time in the universe that we can see, and there is a lot more that not only we cannot see, but as a category, the 'here and now' stands existentially estranged from the elsewhere. Space is transparent and time opens the portal.

The scientific community affirms that when we focus in on the here and now to perceive matter, believe it or not, it's mostly space. This may boggle the mind but the science quantifies that if we were to take all the space out of all the matter that forms the population of human beings, as an example, then you would reduce the overall size of that huge population of peoples to the size of a cube of sugar.[2] I imagine that it is a very heavy cube of compressed matter.

Spacetime is everywhere, and all possibilities or probabilities, should they manifests, exists as phenomena in space and time. Clouds, trees, stars, and all objects of the universe, exists as phenomena in a field of spacetime; but to be apprehended by the senses and experienced as phenomena means that there must be an *observer*. Consciousness therefore, is always required and necessary for reality. I would define consciousness as a relativistic property when time is concentrated in any one space. At some point in time that space is known.

Welcome to the universe. The main criteria for existence include the universe, objects that exist in the universe, and an observer, a watchperson; or, 'consciousness.' The greatest of these is the universe itself, of course, because, the objects and conscious beings in the universe, come from it. But, what of the observer? The observer is very special because we intuitively understand that the universe itself is the ultimate observer; 'Watcher' over all, as it dreams up new ideas.

The observer property, or 'consciousness,' is a very significant and special attribute of the universe. As an observer, I wonder if the cosmos has an overall shape or form? I am referring specifically to that enlightened philosopher, Yeshua, (Jesus); what he must have meant when he said to the religious leaders of that ancient world that the God who sent him and demonstrated his power to them to bear witness; Jesus said to

---

[2] Atoms are 99.99999999% empty space, https://www.physicsforums.com/threads/what-of-an-atom-is-empty.74297/ accessed 4/7/'16

the religious leaders that they had never heard God's voice at any time "nor seen his *shape*."

"...every scribe which is instructed
unto the Kingdom of Heaven,
...bringeth forth out of his treasure things *new* and *old*."
Matthew 13:52

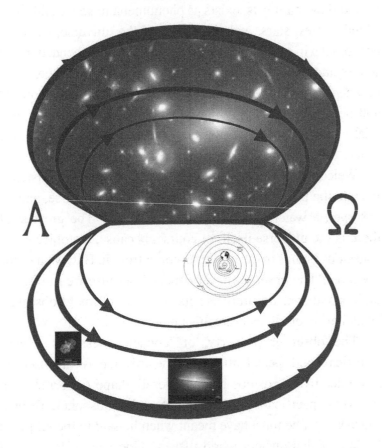

"I AM *Alpha* and *Omega,*
the beginning and the end,
the first and the last."
Revelation 22:13

"The heavens declare the glory of God;
and the firmament sheweth his handiwork.
Day unto day uttereth speech,
and night unto night sheweth knowledge.
There is no speech nor language
where their voice is not heard.
Their *line* is gone out through all the earth,
and their words to the end of the world.
In them hath he set a tabernacle for the sun,"
Psalm 19:1-4

"Is not God in the height of heaven?
and behold the height of the stars,
How high are they?"
Job 22:12

"When I consider thy heavens,
the work of thy fingers,
the moon and stars,
which thou hast ordained;
what is man, that thou art
mindful of him?"
Psalm 8:3,4

We look to the night sky to observe the universe to understand it. During the days, our sight of the universe is obscured by the sun's light but during the night or in the heights, we can peer into, not just the sky, which is as an obscuring palette or plane, but we can literally see through deep space; and, if our tools are up to par, we can see close to the visibility horizon, a moment after the beginning.

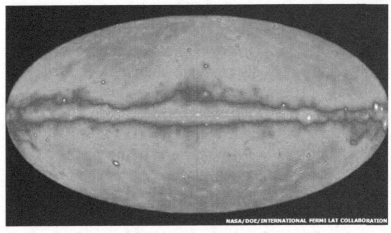

Cosmic Microwave Background Radiation[3]

This iconic map of the cosmic microwave background radiation details an image of the oldest light in the universe. It is essentially a snapshot of the universe when it was just a seed. The science of Cosmology is very mature and our knowledge of the heavens has blossomed. Every living creature that looks up into the heavens at night is a witness—in its own unique way, to an unspoken truth, and a *deep compelling question*. Do you know what that question is?

"I will remember the works of the lord:
surely I will remember thy wonders of old.
I will meditate also of all thy work,
and talk of thy doings.
Thy way, O God, is in the sanctuary:
Who is so great a God as our God?"
Psalm 77:11-13

---

[3] http://lambda.gsfc.nasa.gov/product/cobe/

What captures my imagination most as I think about the ancient biblical texts above are the references to the 'lines' throughout reality, the 'words,' and the language that "in them," i.e., inside these lines and words, *God set the housing for the sun.*

"He stretcheth out the north
over the empty place,
and hangeth the earth upon *nothing,"*
Job 26:7[4]

[4] https://en.wikipedia.org/wiki/Earth's_magnetic_field Glatzmaier, Gary A.; Roberts, Paul H. (1995). "A three-dimensional self-consistent computer simulation of a geomagnetic field reversal". Nature 377 (6546): 203–209. Bibcode:1995Natur.377..203G. doi:10.1038/377203a0

The image above is a three-dimensional computer simulation detailing the Earth's geomagnetic field lines. What I am trying to demonstrate is the understanding that the entire system is in the form of a circuit.

"His going forth is from the end of heaven,
and his circuit unto the ends of it:"
Psalm 19:6

"Thick clouds are a covering to him,
...and he walketh in the circuit of heaven."
Job 22:14

Dark Energy In The Cosmos

Spacetime is the fabric of realities and exist as an invisible, intangible, translucent field composing the Cosmos. Space and time are not material things, but they are conceptual. Spacetime is of the mind, as are all things, and, it exists the very *meaning* of the phrase: the Beginning and the End, *manifested.*

The Universe exists as a solipsistic *'Being'* defined within, inside the words, whose meaning is the 'Beginning and End,' in the same way as the Earth exist between the mirror image poles we call North and South.

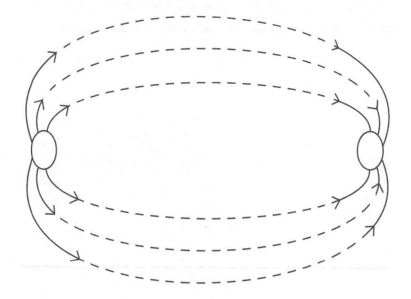

Alpha & Omega exists mirror image poles. The poles exist *simultaneously* in a relationship termed, *positional symmetry (requisite mirror image).*

"I AM ALPHA & OMEGA"

To understand this, visualize the mirror image poles of magnetic fields, as an example. The universe exist between, and encapsulating the poles Alpha and Omega, in the same way the magnetic field exist between and encapsulating its own mirror image poles.

The magnetic field, exist in the form of a circuit in which there is instantaneous communications from pole to pole, uniting them as one. This communication from pole to pole forms the object we call a magnetic field.

Now, if you were to divide a magnet again and again, the poles (requisite mirror image) remain existing in positional symmetry. As a consequence, you would now have multiple magnets that are smaller and smaller in size with their mirror image poles. Extrapolate this principle to the concepts:

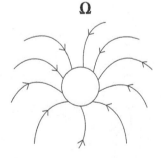

A   **Ω**

&

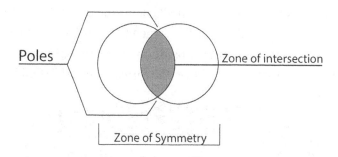

Poles — Zone of intersection

Zone of Symmetry

In the case of the poles the beginning and the end, the spontaneous concept defined in the *intersection of the mirror image poles;* this new idea has the property of "instantaneous communication" between the poles, because they are one. I use the term "intersection" instead of "interaction" because 'intersection' admits mirror image poles without implying that they exist independent of their mutual existence.

The zone of intersection powers the formation of instantaneous lines of communications uniting the poles as one. The circuit is closed. The poles interact in a mutual embrace and something new is generated from this relativity.

In the case of the beginning and the end, the meaning generated is defined "within and between" the concepts the beginning and the end. The system is a circuit in the shape of a torus.

The inherent nature of the intrinsic meaning in the words Alpha and Omega, has a nature that translates information of a *continuum* from the beginning to the end. In the zone of intersection, it is never quite the end; that would be polarity. This domain by virtue of its inherent nature keeps going and going forming a field in which one must apply requisite mirror image, or both poles simultaneously, to any point of reference in the field.

Like a child who just learned a new concept and is beaming with new insights derived from meaning, in like manner the universe inflates on, ever expanding. The zone of intersection generates an inflating *field-of-spacetime*. The Big Bang!

THE BEGINNING AND THE ENDING

"To whom then will ye liken GOD?
Or what likeness will ye compare unto him?
It is he that...*stretcheth* out the heavens as a curtain,
and *spreadeth* them out as a tent to dwell in:"
Isaiah 40:18,22

"Which alone *spreadeth out the heavens*,
and treadeth upon the waves of the sea.
Which maketh Arcturus, Orion, and Pleiades,
and the *chambers of the south*.
Which doeth great things past finding out;
Yea, and wonders without number."
Job 9:8-10

These profound cosmological observations from ancient mystical texts, disclose meaningful insights into an aspect of reality that science only recognized as an existing phenomenon, in the early 1980's. We now understand that the universe is not just expanding but it is accelerating; not like it is stretching, it is spreading out as if the spacetime is upwelling. This is the phenomenon we call dark energy.

Dark energy is the name given by the scientific community to the most potent force observed in the universe. Dark energy is like a fountain emitting spacetime that spreads out spacetime and composes over 73% of the universe's fundamental powers.[5]

"When I consider thy heavens, the work of
thy fingers, the moon and stars, which thou
hast ordained; what is man, that thou art
mindful of him?"
Psalm 8:3,4

"The heavens are thine, the earth also is thine:
as for the world and *the fullness* thereof,
thou hast founded them.
The north and south thou hast created them."
Psalm 89:11,12

The domain between Alpha and Omega, is infinite and ever expanding by its inherent nature because the poles exist *simultaneously*. Alpha and Omega are defined in respect to each other via a closed circuit formed in the "instantaneous communication" between the poles. The phenomenon of "instantaneous communications" between mirroring properties has been affirmed in the scientific community where it is known as *quantum entanglement*.[6]

The field manifest in a domain of resonance, radiating outward indefinitely, expanding, encompassing, defining, and manifesting the very meaning, the very idea:

---

[5] Whittle, M., *Cosmology: The History and Nature of Our Universe*, Parts 1-3, 2008, p20

[6] Greene, B., *The Fabric of the Cosmos :Space, Time, and The Texture of Reality*, 2006, p180.

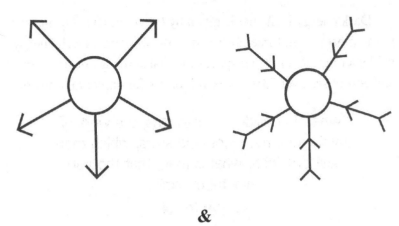

&

The beginning (Alpha) and the end (Omega) is a purely abstract concept, and, a conscious perception. The beginning is as an open portal from which existing things manifest, *in phases*. The end stems from the beginning but its nature leads to increasingly constricted space. These areas where the space becomes increasingly constricted are known as galaxies. Here the spacetime leads directly to the end. Gravity is the law there.

Throughout the universe we see multiple instances of this constricted spacetime (the ending) leading to the end because the nature of the end is so constricted and limited to the here and now. As a result, the end is as a closing pit. The universe is huge and spacetime is unlimited, so we see many many galaxies because the nature of 'end' is very finite.

The beginning and the end, when tied together, is purely abstract. *It is an idea.* Spacetime is its substance. As a graph to the X, and Y axes; so is the spacetime matrix which is the Cosmos, to Alpha and Omega.

Events, objects, entities, etc. all originate from the(ir) beginning; and manifest in space and time. This is the God of Abraham, who is invisible, omnipotent, and the creator of all. God—the body of heaven in his clearness.

17

In Hindu philosophy, "the Vedic sages declared, *'Aham Brahmasmi'*, which can be translated as 'I am the universe' or 'I am everything.'[7] Given this scenario, and accepting the premise that humans, and presumably all things, are made in God's image, then, perhaps space represents the female aspect of God; and time is masculine. Space is the birthing womb, and time—we intuitively speak of father time—it judges and defines.

"While we look not at the things which are seen,
but the things which are not seen:
for the things which are seen are temporal;
but the things which are not seen
are eternal."

2 Corinthians 4:18

The universe has a dual quality that can be reduced to void and matter. The "things which are seen," refers to 'material objects' in the universe. We are advised to not focus on material reality, but this is counterintuitive, because well, first of all, matter is accessible to us, whereas, anyone can just stare into the sky (the void).

We have had considerable success focusing on material objects; that is what science is about. And, since we are social beings living in a capitalist society: the product of science and capitalism is consumerism and technology. Technology refers to the works of our own hands, which we seem to love and idolize. You might remember idolatry, it is when people have such inordinate love and affections towards themselves to the point that they worship the works of their own hands.

---

[7] Chopra, Deepak *"Consciousness as Fundamental Reality"* article presented at the Science of Consciousness Convention, U. of AZ, 2016

Curiously, we are advised to focus on *"the things which are not seen,"* referring to the void, the immaterial nature of reality, which is spiritual, and now we can translate intelligibly to refer to the celestial.

'For the invisible things of him
from the creation of the world
are clearly *seen*,
being understood by the things that are made,
even his eternal power and Godhead;
so they are without excuse."

Romans 1:20

The "invisible things of God" that can be clearly seen from creation, refers to the expanse of space and time itself, that is the cosmos. This is what happens when sentient beings look up at the heavens in wonder at night. The spacetime continuum is enthralling, and its presence has deep fundamental inescapable meaning.

"Canst thou by searching find out God?
Canst thou find out the Almighty unto perfection?
It is as high as heaven; what canst thou do?
Deeper than hell; what canst thou know?"

Job 11:7-9

"I will remember the works of the lord:
surely I will remember thy wonders of old.
I will meditate also of all thy work,
and talk of thy doings.
Thy way, O God, is in the sanctuary:
who is so great a God as our God?"

Psalm 77:11

The Primordial Cosmic Pit

Sombrero Galaxy • M104

Hubble
Heritage

NASA and The Hubble Heritage Team (STScI/AURA) • Hubble Space Telescope ACS • STScI-PRC03-28

"Where wast thou when I laid the
foundation of the earth?
Declare, if thou hast understanding.
Who hath laid the measures thereof, if thou knowest?
Or who hath stretched the line upon it?
Whereupon are the foundations thereof fastened?
Or who laid the cornerstone thereof;
when the morning stars sang together,

and all the sons of God shouted for joy?
...Knowest thou the ordinances of heaven?
Canst thou set the dominion thereof in the earth?
Canst thou *bind the sweet influences of* Pleides,
or loose the bands of Orion?
Canst thou bring forth Mazzaroth in his season?
Or canst thou guide Arcturus with his sons?"

Job 38:4-7,33,31,32

We human beings are physical creatures made of the dust of stars and formed by the universe using gravity and its mirror image side called, acceleration. The power in the phenomenon we call gravity (acceleration) is referred to as dark matter in science and in the the western spiritual paradigm, it is the source behind the *Fall*.

We are very special because we are conscious physical beings endowed with the amazing ability to not just see and experience the world all around us, but, to formulate original thoughts representing reality. We are sentient among all the things that are *somehow* made in the universe. We are not just able to sense the objects in our environment through touch, sight, hearing, tasting, and smell; but, by using symbols and language we are able to conceive them and thus conceive new ideas not just explaining the world around us; but, often recreating the world all around us. This is literally true, is it not? We have the technology to create virtual reality.

The Earth, and all existing things that can be seen throughout the solar system and beyond, throughout the galaxy, and beyond; we see that the universe is mostly space with intermittent areas made of galaxies. The spaces where galaxies exists, displays a very different and contrary nature relative to the expansive nature of deep outer space and the universe as a whole. The space here is very constrictive and characterized by gravity. Gravity is the law here; its power pulls whatever existing thing that comes under its influence, down and inward to increasingly constricted dimensions. The end.

"He looketh upon men, and if any say,
I have sinned, and perverted that which was right,
and it profited me not;
He will deliver his soul from going into the **pit**,
and his life shall see light...
to be enlightened with the light of the living."
Job 33:27,28,30

"Let my prayer come before thee:
incline thine ear unto my cry;
for my soul is full of troubles:
and my life draweth nigh unto the grave.
I am counted with them that go down into the **pit**...
free among the dead, like the slain
that lie in the *grave*...
thou hast laid me in the lowest **pit**,
in darkness, in the *deeps*."
Psalm 88: 2-6

"Hear me speedily, O lord:
my spirit faileth: hide not thy face from me,
lest I be like unto them that go down into the **pit**.
Psalm 143:7

"For the grave cannot praise thee,
death can not celebrate thee:
they that go down into the pit cannot hope
for the truth."
Isaiah 38:18

"Deliver me out of the mire,
and let me not sink; let me be delivered from
them that hate me, and *out of the deep waters*...
neither let the deep swallow me up,
and let not the pit shut her mouth upon me."
Psalm 69:1,15

The meaning in the words, "let not the pit shut her mouth upon me," elicits in the amateur cosmologist in me an understanding consistent with western science. We understand that the black hole is delineated by the 'event horizon.' The event horizon marks a line of demarcation in spacetime; beyond which, even light cannot escape. Once you've crossed that threshold, the mouth is shut.

"But GOD shall wound the head of his enemies,
and the hairy scalp of such an one
as goeth on still in his tresspasses...
I will bring my people again *from the* depths of the sea:"
Psalm 68:21,22

"Thou shalt forget thy misery; and remember it as
waters that pass away."
Job 11:16

We see here how freely our ideas of water and spacetime are interchangeable in the realm of metaphysical spirituality. The imagery is that of the tale of our past lives, which was very concrete in the moment when lived, but in passing, it is like the waters of a river flown bye.

"O Lord, thou has brought up my soul
from the grave: thou hast kept me alive,
that I should not go down into the pit.
Psalm 30:30

"As for thee also, by the blood of thy covenant
I have sent forth thy prisoners out of *the pit*
wherein there is no water.
Turn you to the strong hold,
ye prisoners of hope:
even to day do I declare that I will render
double unto thee;
Zechariah 9:11,12

The concept of the 'pit' represents a very serious event of gravity with so much constrictive pull moving toward the most finite limits of the universe, that there is very little *spacetime* or *water* down there. And where there is no water, there is only fire.

"And the fifth angel sounded,
and I saw a star fall from heaven unto the earth:
and to him was given the key of the bottomless pit.
And he opened the bottomless pit;
and there arose a smoke out of the pit,
as the smoke of a great furnace;

and the sun and the air were darkened
by reason of the smoke of the pit."
Revelation 9:1-2

"I made the nations to shake at the sound of his fall,
when I cast him down to hell
with them that descend down into the pit:"
Ezekiel 31:16

"And I saw an angel come down from heaven,
having the key of the bottomless pit
and a great chain in his hand.
And he laid hold on the dragon, that old serpent,
which is the Devil, and Satan,
and bound him a thousand years,
and cast him into the bottomless pit,
and shut him up, and set a seal upon him,
that he should not deceive the nations no more..."
Revelation 20: 1-3

Word

"In the beginning was the *Word,*
and the *Word* was with **GOD,**
and the *Word* was **GOD.**"

John 1:1

Imagine a wave on the open sea. The body of that wave, its' form, carries energy (information) that is a part of, yet distinct from the sea. The wave has a shape and a form that differentiates it from the surrounding water.

Words are as waves in the ocean. Words are defined by their meanings, and, the letters or sounds, provides form. Different sounds can have the same meaning (languages), and the same sound can have different meanings (context, body language, etc.). The sound of a word, or the written symbols, vary universally; yet all varieties of ways of symbolizing ideas can refer to the same reality. Hence, we are able to translate foreign languages, facilitating understanding.

The conscious and subconscious perceptions of reality are determined primarily in the 'meanings' of words. 'Meaning,' is inherent and intrinsic to each word, and we attach 'meaning,' and meaning comes pre-attached to what we see, taste, smell, or otherwise sense. But what is the nature of meaning?

Meaning requires consciousness to be perceived. Meaning, therefore, is tied to psychological states of consciousness.

The sound like the letters (letters form the sound, etc.), are merely symbols that refer to the different types of meanings intrinsic to each word. The meaning, in turn, applies directly to reality. For example, if I invoke the word 'tree'; this word has a sound and spelling for form, but meaning guides us to the reality. So when I say the word 'tree,' this guides the conscious mind to an existing thing that embodies the idea, 'tree.' Again, if I were to use a totally different sound and say, *el arbol;* this word has a different sound and spelling yet it's meaning refers to the same tree.

Thus, it is primarily in the interactions of the meanings of words in the mind that we map reality. Consciousness creates reality via the interaction of meaningful thoughts.

The spoken word is emitted as a wave of energy (information = symbol + meaning) in the spacetime continuum. We know today that energy is transmuted to matter via the formula, $e = mc^2$. The body of that wave, i.e., the energy that defines it from the rest of the sea, is under the veneer of the surface (invisible); this is the very meaning of that word. It is from this invisible "stuff," that the visible (material world) is manifested, beginning at the most finite scales in space and time.

"By the word of the Lord were the heavens made:
and all the host of them by the breath of his mouth."
Psalm 33:6

"...the ages were created by a *word* from God,
so that from the invisible
the visible world came to be."
Hebrews 11:3

The meaning aspect of words, this is the spirit, or energy, the *feeling* or vibe of that **wor*(l)*d**. The spirit world, which is mystical, dwells inside domains of the *meanings* of things. Reality is played out in spatial dimensions, which includes concepts of scale and relativity.

The material world exists and correlates to the letters. Letters form the sound, and are quanta. The spoken-word, incorporates sound and meaning.

The meaning aspect of words, are often multi-dimensional and multifaceted. Also, there are hidden domains of meanings, dependent on the observer's level of understanding of context.

There are higher levels of understanding, and lower levels. Individual listeners may perceive aspects of the meaning(s); with other aspects hidden entirely, depending on their personal experiences and intelligences.

These dynamic perceptions that are all functions of consciousness, creates chambers of meanings, layers of meanings, and blind spots, depending on the observer's conscious maturity.

The meaning aspect of words, this is the fundamental "stuff" of reality; *the very space and time.* If words paint pictures, the meaning is the paint—including the color of the paint; the brush is the tongue.

"The words of a man's mouth are as deep waters, and the wellspring of wisdom as a flowing brook."
Proverbs 18:4

The meaning of the phrase the beginning and the ending—its nature is ever expanding, continuum, infinite: this is a *spirit*. We exist within this infinite, ever expanding continuum; which exist the very meaning of the words Alpha & Omega. We call this continuum space and time. It is the cosmic ocean.

The scientific community recently provided and confirmed empirical evidence of ripples in the cosmic ocean, indicating that spacetime is *real* because it serves as the medium through which, these waves called, gravity waves,[8] flow.

According to observations of cosmologist, beyond 200 million light years from the here and now, all that we can see of the universe is clear translucent spacetime.[9]

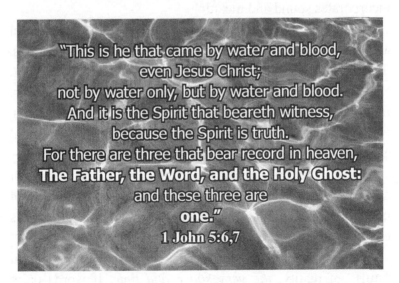

"This is he that came by water and blood, even Jesus Christ; not by water only, but by water and blood. And it is the Spirit that beareth witness, because the Spirit is truth. For there are three that bear record in heaven, The Father, the Word, and the Holy Ghost: and these three are one."
1 John 5:6,7

---

[8] http://www.nytimes.com/2016/02/12/science/ligo-gravitational-waves-black-holes-einstein.html?_r=0

[9] Whittle, M., *Cosmology*, 14

These remarkable words inform us of a profound and meaningful concept; that Jesus came to the Earth by traveling through spacetime (water) and entered our world as a human being through birth (blood).

"And the Word was made flesh, and dwelt among us,
(and we beheld his glory,
the glory as of the only begotten of the Father),
full of grace and truth."
1 John 1:14

"Jesus *cried* and said, he that believeth on me,
believeth not on me,
but on *him that sent me.*
And he that seeth me seeth *him that sent me.*
I AM come a light into the world,
that whosoever believeth on me
should not abide in darkness."
John 12:44-45

"But the hour cometh, and now is,
when the true worshippers shall worship the Father
in *spirit* and in **truth**: for the Father seeketh
such to worship him. GOD is a spirit:
and they that worship him
must worship him in spirit and in truth."
John 4:23-24

Are you a Christian, a Buddhist, a Hindu, a Muslim, or maybe of another religious persuasion; consider becoming a true worshipper. Clearly, if you call yourself a Christian, then you would speak of the, I AM. Jesus, who represents I

AM perfectly, made it very clear that this story was not about himself. It is about his father, who is I AM.

I would not advise anyone to ignore the 'truth' requirement in understanding the word here. Anyone can worship God in spirit. That is what organized religion is all about. It's a show.

To worship God in truth means not just a show or ceremony put on by desperate and corrupt people, but also, an actual relationship where we interact directly with the divine, and the divine is manifested in power in the lives of these people—who are the children of God.

I guess that the bottom line is in this, that the true worshippers are not desperate, because, they are in divine communion with the very source of, not just life, but all reality. They themselves are alive, thriving, social, loving, righteous, and truthful.

But what of the 'believers' who are accustomed to bathing themselves in religious robes and services? How will they respond in the day that God manifest again fulfilling prophecy? The one's who call themselves Christians, they are saying that "the antichrist is coming;" if it is so, then it is because GOD is coming.

Water ≈ The Cosmic Ocean

"I am Alpha and Omega, the beginning and the end.
I will give unto him that is athirst of the
fountain of the water of life freely.
He that overcometh shall inherit all things;
and I will be his God,
and he shall be my son."
Revelation 21: 6-7

The concept of a primordial "fountain of the water of life," is deeply appealing to me, and I would think, to any thoughtful soul. I wonder why we do not hear more about this amazing idea? I suppose that the story of Ponce de Leon's search for the rumored fountain-of-life, can be traced back to this ancient mystical concept. There is a whole lot to be mined here.

If we accept the premise, as many people worldwide do, that water metaphorically translates to the cosmic ocean; then we have the idea of a fountain that emits spacetime. Earlier, I alluded to the concept of dark energy, which the scientific community recognizes as the most powerful fundamental agent of the universe, responsible for over 73% of the universe's overall fundamental properties.[10]

---

[10] Whittle, *cosmology,* 18

As an individual earnestly seeking to find a way in this "between" life and death status of time, I find that in learning of such amazing concepts as 'dark energy,' as a real fundamental constituent of the universe; I am intrigued and I wonder, what is dark energy?

Dark energy is the name given by the scientific community to a feature of the universe that explains its expansion. The existence of dark energy is assumed to be real via an act of reason, however, the scientific community acknowledges that 'dark energy' itself has never been seen. What we see are its effects on the universe, expanding and infusing space between galaxies throughout the cosmos.

Dark energy's presence and power is so dominant, it is very clear to the scientific community that the expansion of the universe overcomes the contracting potential of the gravity that is associated with the other dominant constituent of the universe, known as dark matter.

Again, we have never seen dark matter but its existence is assumed to be very real via an act of reason, as evidenced by its gravitational affects within galaxies. Dark matter accounts for about 23% of the universe' ultimate powers.[11]

So it appears that we have two dominant fundamental powers of the universe in the form of dark energy and dark matter whose mutual presence constitutes over 96% of the universe's fundamental, empirical, powers.

The rest of the constituents of the universe include ordinary matter, photons, etc. The material objects that come into being in the universe are temporal; which is to say that they have a beginning, and we understand from experience that at some time, all 'things' come to an end.

---

[11] Ibid, 20

This is a reference to the *'arrow of time.'*[12] Time moves in a direction from past to future because time moves in the *circuit* from the beginning to the end. Even the suns of the galaxies, as powerful as they are, are birthed into existence in some place and time, and eventually burn out and come to an end, in a myriad of chaotic ways.

Existing objects of the universe come into being as ordered things. The beginning is an event of high order. The end is disorder. The end of an ordered being is in disorder; which can manifest in a myriad of ways including disease, accidents, war, etc. The words, the *Beginning,* and the *End,* defines the existence of things. The concept, the "Beginning and the End," is God.

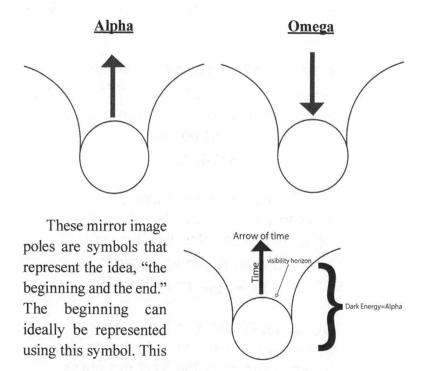

Alpha

Omega

These mirror image poles are symbols that represent the idea, "the beginning and the end." The beginning can ideally be represented using this symbol. This

[12] Greene, B., *The Fabric of the Cosmos,* p537

graphic is very significant in terms of the content of meaningful information. When we unpack the word, 'beginning,' it is as a fountain emitting space and time (spacetime), this accounts for dark energy.

When we, who dwell in the here and now of spacetime (the finite, near the end), look up into the heavens to see spacetime, what we see is the past; so consider the arrow of time, though moving forward, we see only the past.

This observation alludes to a retrograde motion to our concepts of spacetime that potentially may provide the vacuum energy as a bow in an arrow, for inflation. Notice that the *emergence horizon* of the Alpha pole serves as the *visibility horizon* for the beings who exists within the universe and came into existence after the big bang. The Alpha pole is dark energy, the primordial "fountain of the water of life."

"For my people have committed two evils;
they have forsaken me the *fountain of living waters*,
and hewed them out cisterns, broken cisterns,
That can hold no water."
Jeremiah 2:13

"O Lord, the hope of Israel,
all that forsake thee shall be ashamed,
...because they have forsaken the Lord,
the *fountain of living waters*."
Jeremiah 17:13

"Thy mercy, O Lord, is in the heavens;
and thy faithfulness reacheth unto the clouds.
Thy righteousness is like the great mountains;
Thy judgments are a great deep:

O Lord, thou preservest man and beast.
How excellent is thy loving kindness, O GOD!
Therefore the children of men put their trust
under the shadow of thy wings.
They shall be abundantly satisfied with
the fatness of thy house;
and thou shalt make them drink of
the river of thy pleasures.
For with thee is the *fountain of life:*
in thy light shall we see light."

Psalm 36:5-9

The Alpha pole is responsible not just for expanding the universe, but coincidentally, it explains and reconciles many of the amazing discoveries that we have of the universe in the world of science. The Alpha pole details the nature of dark energy, accounts for the visibility horizon that is a veil that prevents us from seeing the beginning at time zero; it also explains the arrow of time as a consequence of the direction of the circuit generated in the instantaneous communication between mirror image poles. The circuit has flow and direction. Time runs from the beginning to the end in the same way that gravity lines run from the South pole to the North pole, of planetary bodies.

"I AM Alpha and Omega,
the first and the last...
Fear not; **I AM** the first and the last:
I AM he that liveth, and was dead;
And, behold, **I AM** alive for evermore, Amen;
and have the keys of hell and of death."

Revelation 1:11,17,18

Lets think about what is first, and also last? Well, if some thing exist, then it is for at least a few moments of time; in some place. Space and Time are prerequisite for existence because, it provides the context and the backdrop for the development of 'being.' Space and time must exist first, and also, last; because the story continues even when the end comes for existing things. The show must go on so the ongoing context remains existant.

Spacetime is our conscious experience of the omnipresent invisible GOD of Abraham. Spacetime is the *waters of life* because all probabilities require space and time to manifest and play out their being.

"Praise ye the Lord. Praise ye the
Lord from the heavens:
praise him in the heights.
Praise ye him, all his angels: praise ye him, all his hosts.
Praise ye him, sun and moon:
Praise him all ye stars of light.
Praise him, ye heavens of heavens, *and ye waters*
that be above the heavens."
Psalm 148:1-4

I hope that you are able to appreciate the deep field insights provided by these ancient philosophers and seers. The reference to the waters above in the heavens points to spacetime itself and is readily appreciated metaphorically but more interesting, it is a scientific fact that there is literally an abundance of water in the cosmos.

"He hath compassed *the waters* with bounds,
until the day and night come to an end.
The pillars of heaven tremble

and are astonished at his reproof.
By his spirit he hath garnished the heavens;
his hand hath formed the *crooked serpent.*
Lo, these are parts of his way:
but how little a portion is heard of him?"

Job 26:10,11,13,14

Spacetime has such dynamic properties as it slips up (spacetime) or down (water) the metaphorical ladder. Spacetime is defined by cycles to the extent that day and night, the mirror-image components of a full 'day,' are discerned.

Eagle Nebula Hubble Space Telescope

"The pillars of heaven tremble and are astonished at his reproof," has cartoon-like imagery. Imagine gigantic (think cosmic scale) pillars trembling in the presence of God. Know that the spacetime itself is all alive because it is all of consciousness. So what we would ordinarily conceive as inanimate objects well, consider that not just the objects but the very spacetime providing the immediate context; all is consciousness. All is, I AM!

When God (presumably the person of God) walks through an area in the heavens, all of the environment is alive and conscious everywhere, thus the pillars are astonished when in the presence of God.

"By his spirit he hath garnished the heavens," simply means that God decorated the heavens by thinking about it and doing it according to his liking.

I wonder what the crooked serpent refers to, I think that is likely a reference to the Milky Way. Yes, of course, the waters (spacetime) and the crooked serpent (galaxies); the Alpha and Omega.

"...I will come on thee as a thief,
and thou shalt not know
what hour I will come upon thee...
He that overcometh,
the same shall be clothed in white raiment;
and I will not blot out his name
out of the **book of life,**
but I will confess his name before my Father,
and before his angels.
He that hath an ear let him hear
what the *spirit* saith unto the churches...
As many as I love, I rebuke and chasten:
be zealous therefore, and repent.

Behold, I stand at the door, and knock:
if any man hear my voice, and open the door,
I will come in to him, and will sup with him,
and he with me."
Revelation 3:3,5,6,19,20

"But the Lord is the true **GOD,** he is the living **GOD.**
and an everlasting king:
at his wrath the earth shall tremble,
and the nations shall not be able
to abide his indignation.
He hath made the earth by his power,
he hath established the world by his wisdom,
and hath stretched out
the heavens by his discretion.
When he uttereth his voice,
There is a *multitude of waters* in the heavens."
Jeremiah 10:10,12,13

When God speaks, a lot of spacetime is emitted
into the cosmic ocean.

"Touching the Almighty, we cannot find him out:
...Hast thou with him spread out the sky,
which is like a *molten looking glass?"*
Job 37:23,18

Egg Nebula · CRL 2688   HST · WFPC2
PRC96-03 · ST ScI OPO · January 16, 1996
R. Sahai and J. Trauger (JPL), the WFPC2 Science Team and NASA

"Bless the Lord, O my soul.
O Lord my GOD, thou art very great;
thou art clothed with honour and majesty.
Who coverest thyself with *light* as with a garment:
who *stretchest out the heavens like a curtain:*
who **layeth the beams of his chambers** *in the waters...*
Who laid the foundations of the earth...
Thou coverest it with the *deep* as with a garment:
the waters stood above the mountains."

Psalm 104:1-3,6

The text above simply tells us to bless God with all our hearts and souls because God is very great. The person of God is majestic and uses light for clothing. GOD is the force that inflates the universe filing it with spacetime. God's house has great big beams firmly planted in the cosmos.

God also laid the foundations of the Earth, which is so low—from the universe's perspective, that from heaven's perspective, *the Earth is covered by the deep.* But from the Earth's perspective, we see spacetime above and below and throughout the heavens.

"For this shall everyone that is Godly pray unto thee
in a time when thou mayest be found:
surely in the *floods of great waters*
they shall not come nigh unto him."
Psalm 32:6

When we think of GOD, we must think of GOD in two ways: one, GOD as the whole; also, God as a person. In the Western tradition, Jesus represents God as a person, but simultaneously, we know that Jesus referred to his Father as GOD.

What we see in the text above is that people will be and have been praying and calling upon God throughout the ages, until a time when God is willing to answer the phone. The problem lies in that GOD is infinite so how can the finite hope to reach the ears of God.

"He made darkness his secret place;
his pavilion round about him were dark waters
and thick clouds of the skies."
Psalm18:11

42

"Then shall we know, if we follow on to know the Lord:
his going forth is prepared as the morning;
and he shall come unto us as the *rain,*
as the latter and former *rain* unto the earth."

Hosea 6:3

When it rains, the water congeals out of the atmosphere and falls from the sky onto the Earth. When we look at a large pool of water, what do we see? We see a reflection of the heavens above, and the surrounding environment. The water reflects information of the world from which it came. Water is analog of spacetime.

We can see the life-giving power of water and its remarkable properties very literally in the transformation of the Earth, in its regions where it had been bone dry; then, when the rain comes, streams begin to flow, grass pops up, the complex sounds of life become a cacophony and vibrant life is manifests. Living creatures emerge from everywhere including sometimes directly from the dirt itself, where some creatures can rest in senescence till the rains come. Life manifests and flourishes in the interrelationship between dirt and water.

The spiritual translation, which is metaphor, informs us that God will come in the form of rain (condensed spacetime) and the *meaning* in these waters will spread out like evaporate to create a new spirit which composes the history to come.

"He shall come down like *rain* upon the mown grass:
as *showers* that *water* the earth:"

Psalm 72:6

43

"The voice of thy thunder was in the heaven:
the lightenings lightened the world:
the earth trembled and shook.
Thy way is in the sea, and thy path *in the great waters,*
and thy footsteps are *not known."*

Psalm 77:18,19

"Now unto the King eternal, immortal, *invisible,*
the only wise **GOD,**
be honour and glory for ever and ever. Amen."

1 Timothy 1:17

"Blessed be thou, Lord GOD of Israel our Father,
for ever and ever.
Thine, O Lord, is the greatness, and the power,
and the glory, and the victory, and the majesty:
for all that is in the heaven and in the earth is *thine;*
thine is the kingdom, O Lord,
and thou art exalted as head above all."

1 Chronicles 29:10-11

The Name Of God

"Who hath ascended up into heaven, or descended?
Who hath gathered the wind in his fist?
Who hath *bound the waters in a garment?*
Who hath established all the ends of the earth?
What is his **name,** and what is his **son's name,**
If thou canst tell?"
Proverbs 30:4

Imagine if something had the power to collect the wind in its' fist; if so, perhaps it is because it is about to throw it, so watch out for hurricanes and other whirlwinds! "Who hath bound the waters in a garment," may seem as a very obscure or esoteric concept, however, it is an event that most of us have already seen. When we see pictures of galaxies, we are seeing spacetime that has been folded, like fabric rung into the shape of a ginormous 4-dimensional spiral.

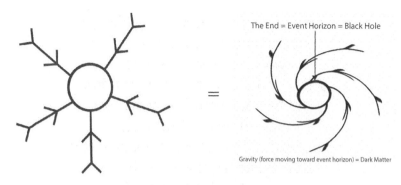

"And I turned to see the voice that spake with me.
And being turned, I saw seven golden candle sticks;
And in the midst of the seven candlesticks *One*
like unto the Son of man,
clothed with a garment down to the foot,

and girt about the paps with a golden girdle.
His head and hairs were white like
wool, as white as snow;
and his eyes were as a *flame* of fire;
...his feet like unto fine brass as if
they burned in a furnace;
and his voice as the sound of many *waters*.
...his countenance was as the sun
shineth in his strength."

Revelation 1:12-16

Let us use poetic license to visualize this remarkable scenario described above. We are going to imagine this highly stylized dramatic scene in which an earthling meets up with what is ostensibly, the person of GOD. The king's voice is very deep and contains dramatic creative power. Imagine a James Earl Jonesesque voice with the sound and power of Niagara Falls in the background.

The messiah is wearing light as clothing down to his feet. His skin shining like fine brass is consistent with our ideas of people from the Middle East. Take the tone of a typical Mid-Eastern person but make the olive skin to shine.

The imagery of burning in an oven indicates perhaps a darker look approaching the bottom of the feet, then red-hot at the soles of the foot. I imagine the soles of his feet bright red, as if heated by an oven. His eyes are each like a soft flame, in a face of bright light. His hair is like wool, white as snow.

"For now we see through a glass, **darkly;**
but then face to face:
now I know in part;
but then shall I know even as also **I AM** known."

1 Corinthians 13:12

I find this scripture to be intriguingly obtuse unless you
understand simply that God is I AM. Then suddenly this obtuse
sentence makes perfect simple sense.

"And Moses said unto God,
behold, when I come unto the children of Israel,
and shall say unto them,
The God of your fathers hath sent me unto you;
and they shall say unto me, **what is his name?**
What shall I say unto them?
And GOD said unto Moses,
I AM THAT I AM:
and he said, thus shalt thou say
unto the children of Israel,
I AM hath sent me unto you.
...this is my name forever,
and this is my memorial unto all generations."

Exodus 3:13-15

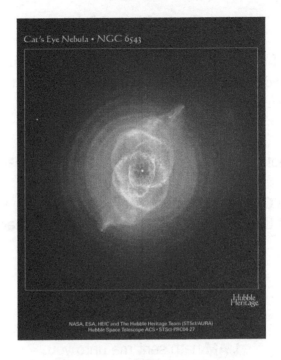

Cat's Eye Nebula • NGC 6543

Hubble Heritage

NASA, ESA, HEIC and The Hubble Heritage Team (STScI/AURA)
Hubble Space Telescope ACS • STScI-PRC04-27

"Thus saith **GOD** the **LORD,**
he that created the heavens,
and stretched them out;
he that spread forth the earth,
and that which cometh out of it;
he that giveth breath unto the people upon it,
and spirit to them that walk therein:
I the Lord have called thee in righteousness,
and will hold thine hand, and will keep thee,
and give thee a covenant of the people,
for a light of the Gentiles;
To open the blind eyes,
to bring out the *prisoners* from the *prison*,
and them that sit in darkness out of the *prison* house...
I AM the Lord: that is my name...

49

and my glory will I not give to another,
neither my praise to graven images.
Sing unto the lord a new song,
and his praise to the end of the earth...
Let them give glory unto the Lord,
and declare his praise in the islands.
The Lord shall go forth as a might man,
he shall stir up jealousy like a man of war:
he shall cry, yeah, roar;
he shall prevail against his enemies."

Isaiah 42:5-8,10,12-13

Contrary to conservative standards and the behaviors we see in historical and contemporary religion, it appears that the God of Abraham has deep empathy for the individuals in our societies, who find themselves oppressed, condemned, and imprisoned. The plight of the prisoner appears to be of deep concern to God and this fact flies in the face of contemporary religion, which tends to be conservative.

The proponents of our religious society tend to promote increased incarcerations, particularly for people of color, and other minorities. Jesus warned that though he himself will not judge, there is still one that judgeth, and his words will ultimately judge and reprove us.

This means that when the times come and we see GOD's spirit again in the Earth, then those individuals who live their lives astray from the path of life will experience difficulties to remember to change course. The word says that we will all be judged according to how we have judged each other. So if you are liberal toward others, you will be liberally judged. If you judge harshly, you will be judged harshly.

"...and they shall know **THAT I AM** the **LORD.**
So will I make *my holy name* known
in the midst of my people Israel;
and I will not let them pollute my holy name any more:
and the heathen shall know **THAT I AM the LORD,**
the **Holy One** in Israel."
Ezekiel 39:6,7

"Therefore my people shall know **my name:**
therefore my people shall know *in that day*
THAT I AM he that doth speak:
behold it is I."
Isaiah 52:6

"...if then I be a Father, where is mine honour?
And if I be a master, where is my fear?`
Saith the Lord of hosts, unto you, **O priest**
that *despise my name.*
Malachi 1:6

"...**I AM** a great king and my **name**
is dreadful among the heathen.
...For from the rising of the sun
unto the going down of the same,
my **name** shall be great among the Gentiles;
and in every place incense shall be offered
unto my **name,** and a pure offering:
for my **name** shall be great
among the heathen, saith the Lord of hosts.
But ye have profaned it..."
Malachi 1:14,11,12

The names **JeHoVaH,** or **YaHWeH,** are both derived off **YHVH.** This Hebrew word, **YHVH,** is the sacred name of the 'consciousness' that is **Alpha & Omega.** To speak this name in whatever language that you use, is to intone the words that mean, "**I AM** that **I AM.**" I wonder if a more accurate interpretation is **"I AM** the **I AM."**

It is the traditions of our religious leaders to refer to **YHVH (JeHoVaH,** or **YaHWeH),** in a manner that ignores the "**I AM**" meaning. **YHVH** is often times translated, **"the Lord,"** which it is.

The priests in times past reasoned that the sacred name of God is too holy to intone among men. Without regard to their intent, the effect is to obscure the meaning in God's name. Some people even refer to **YHVH** as, "the tetragrammaton," or the four letters.

To speak God's name, if you are English speaking is to intone the words, "**I AM.**" The word, "**I AM,**" is God's sacred name; the name of the invisible God of Israel who is the Father of Yeshua (Jesus), and the God of Moses.

"...O Lord, revive thy work in the midst of the years,
in the midst of the years make known;
in wrath remember mercy.

God came from Teman,
and the Holy One from mount Paran. Selah.
His glory covered the heavens,
and the earth was full of his praise.
And his brightness was as the light...
Before him went the pestilence,
and burning coals went forth at his feet.

He stood, and measured the earth:
he beheld, and drove asunder the nations;
and the everlasting mountains were scattered,
the perpetual hills did bow: his ways are everlasting...

Thou didst march through the land in indignation,
thou didst thresh the heathen in anger.
Thou wentest forth for the salvation of thy people,
even for salvation with thine anointed;
thou woundest the head of the house of the wicked,
by discovering the foundation unto the neck. Selah.

...their rejoicing was as to devour
the poor secretly.

Thou didst walk through the *sea* with thine horses,
through the *heap of great waters.*
When I heard, my belly trembled; my
lips quivered at the voice:
rottenness entered into my bones,
and I trembled in myself,
That I might rest in the day of trouble:
when he cometh onto the people,
he will invade them with his troops."
Habakkuk 3:2-6,12-16

"For GOD will save Zion, and will
build the cities of Judah:
that they may dwell there, and have it in possession.
The seed also of his servants shall inherit it:
and they that love his **name** shall dwell therein."
Psalm 69:35-36

"And in that day shall the deaf hear
the words of the book,
and the eyes of the blind shall see out of obscurity,
and out of darkness.
The meek also shall increase their joy in the Lord,
and the **poor** among men shall rejoice
in the Holy One of Israel.
*For the terrible one is brought to nought,
and the scorner is consumed,
and all that watch for iniquity are cut off:*
That make a man an offender for a word,
and lay a snare for him that reproveth in the gate,
and turn aside the just for a thing of nought.
Therefore thus saith the Lord, who redeemed Abraham
concerning the house of Jacob,
Jacob shall not now be ashamed,
neither shall his face now wax pale.
But when he seeth his children, the work of my hands,
in the midst of him, they shall sanctify my name,
and sanctify the Holy One of Jacob,
and shall fear the GOD of Israel.
*They also that erred in spirit shall
come to understanding,*
and they that *murmured* shall learn doctrine."
Isaiah 29: 18-24

This remarkable scripture conjures up a very meaningful and interesting time in human history. It speaks to a *zeitgeist* when people will read the bible and understand it clearly due to the historical times that they are in. The words will make perfect sense given the context and everyone will agree to the meaning as it applies to their present state of being.

It is evident that the God of the universe feels for the poor and the meek, so they are mentioned to have gained benefits to the extent that they are able to rejoice in the God of Abraham.

"The terrible one who is brought to nought," refers to the rich and powerful who look down on the poor, with scorn; thinking more of themselves than is wise. They are somehow brought to nothing. Perhaps, their money—the source of their power, will mean nothing. They are characterized as having the power and mind to judge others unjustly; condemning people just because they said something they disagree with, or searching through their history to find something they can accuse them of. It also manifest in the power of the media, when the forces of influence direct the media to accuse and condemn, accuse and condemn, even when innocent.

It appears that GOD will change the course of human history to the extent that these typical agents of the 'powers-that-be' will find that they no longer have the agency to influence reality to their own ends. During these times, God will raise up his own children in the Earth who have a mindset to do right seeing all the corruption and inequality, which is the manifest legacy of our forbearers.

This generation will live and they will recognize that the reality that they are living in, is the work of GOD, and they will acknowledge GOD. And the secret conversations between people of society accusing others, will be quieted.

"Among the Gods there is none like unto thee, O Lord;
neither are there any works like unto thy works.
All nations whom thou hast made shall come
and worship before thee, O Lord;
and shall glorify thy name.
For thou art great, and doest wondrous things:
thou art God alone. Teach me thy way, O Lord;
I will walk in thy truth: unite my heart to fear thy name.
I will praise thee, O Lord my God, with all my heart:
and I will glorify thy name for evermore.
For great is thy mercy toward me:
and thou hast delivered my soul from the lowest hell."

Psalm 86:8-13

"He that dwelleth in the secret place of the most High
shall abide under the shadow of the Almighty.
I will say of the Lord,
He is my refuge and my fortress;
my God; in him will I trust...
Because thou has made the Lord,
which is my refuge,
even the most High, thy habitation;
There shall no evil befall thee,
neither shall any plague come nigh thy dwelling.
For he shall give his angels charge over thee,
to keep thee in all thy ways.
They shall bear thee up in their hands,
lest thou dash thy foot against a stone...
Because he hath set his love upon me
therefore will I deliver him:
I will set him on high,
because he hath known my **name.**

He shall call upon me, and I will answer him:
I will be with him in trouble;
I will deliver him, and honour him.
With long life will I satisfy him,
And shew him my **salvation.**

Psalm 91:1-2,9-12,14-16

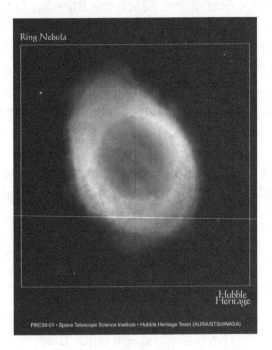

Ring Nebula

Hubble
Heritage

PRC99-01 • Space Telescope Science Institute • Hubble Heritage Team (AURA/STScI/NASA)

"I, even **I, AM** he that blotteth out thy
transgressions *for mine own sake,*
and will not remember thy sins.
Put me in remembrance:
let us plead together:
declare thou, that thou mayest be justified.
Thy first father hath sinned,
and thy teachers have transgressed against me."

Isaiah 43:25-27

"Be still, and know **THAT I AM** God:
I will be exalted among the heathen,
I will be exalted in the earth."

Psalm 46:10

Hourglass Nebula · MyCn18
Hubble Space Telescope · WFPC2

"I AM sought of them that asked not for me;
I AM *found* of them that sought me not:
I said behold me, behold me..."

Isaiah 65:1

"For thus saith the high and lofty One that
inhabiteth eternity, whose name is Holy;
I dwell in the high and holy place, with him also
that is of a contrite and humble spirit,
To revive the spirit of the humble,
and to revive the heart of the contrite ones."

Isaiah 57:15

"Ye are my witnesses, saith the Lord,
and my servant *whom I have chosen*:
that ye may know and believe me, and understand
THAT I AM he:
before me there was no God formed,
neither shall there be after me.
I, even **I, AM** the LORD;
and beside me there is no saviour.
...therefore ye are my witnesses, saith the Lord,
THAT I AM God.
Yea, before the day was **I AM** he...
I AM the Lord, your Holy One,
the creator of Israel,
your King."

Isaiah 43:10-13,15

"And in that day thou shalt say, O Lord,
I will praise thee: though thou wast angry with me,
thine anger is turned away, and thou comfortedst me.
Behold, God is my salvation; I will
trust, and not be afraid:
For the Lord JE-HO'-VAH is my strength and my song;
he also is become my salvation.
Therefore with joy shall ye
draw water out of the wells
of salvation. And in that day shall ye say,
Praise the Lord, call upon his name,
declare his doings among the people,
make mention that his name is exalted.
Sing unto the Lord; for he hath done excellent things:

this is known in all the Earth.
Cry out and shout, thou inhabitant of Zion:
for great is the Holy One of Israel in the midst of thee."

Isaiah 12: 1-6

"At that time they shall call Jerusalem
the throne of the Lord;
and all the nations shall be gathered unto it,
to the **name** of the Lord, to Jerusalem:
neither shall they walk anymore after the *imagination*
of their evil heart.
But I said, how shall I put thee among the children,
and give thee a pleasant land,
a goodly heritage of the hosts of nations?
And I said, thou shalt call me, my Father;
and *shalt not turn away from me.*

Jeremiah 3:17,19

"Acquaint now thyself with him, and be at peace:
thereby good shall come unto thee.
Receive I pray thee, the *law from his mouth,*
and lay up his words in thine heart.
If thou return to the Almighty, thou shalt be built up,
thou shalt put away iniquity far from thy tabernacles.
Then shalt thou lay up gold as the dust,
and the gold of Ophir
as the stones of the brooks.
Yea, the Almighty shall be thy defense,
and thou shalt have plenty of silver.
For then shalt thou have thy delight in the Almighty,
and shalt lift up thy face unto GOD.
Thou shalt make thy prayer unto him,

and he shall hear thee,
and thou shalt pay thy vows.
Thou shalt also decree a thing,
and it shall be established unto thee:
and the light shall shine upon thy ways.
When men are cast down, then thou shalt say,
there is lifting up; and he shall save the humble person.
He shall deliver the island of the innocent:
and it is delivered by the pureness of thine hands."

Job 22:21-30

"Behold, God is great, and *we know him not,*
neither can the number of his years be searched out.
For he maketh small the drops of water:
they pour down rain according to the vapor thereof:
which the clouds do drop and distill
upon man abundantly."

Job 36:26-28

"Hear attentively the noise of his voice,
and the sound that goeth out of his mouth.
He directeth it under the whole heaven,
and his lightening unto the ends of the earth.
After it a voice roareth: he thundereth
with the voice of his
excellency; and he will not stay them
when his voice is heard.
GOD thundereth marvelously with his voice;
Great things doeth he, which we cannot comprehend.
For he saith to the snow, be thou on the earth;
likewise to the small rain,
and to the great rain of his strength...

Dost thou know the balancing of the clouds,
the wondrous works of him which
is perfect in knowledge?

Touching the Almighty, we cannot find him out.
he is excellent in power, and in judgment, and in plenty
of justice: he will not afflict.
Men do therefore fear him:
he respecteth not any that are wise of heart."

Job 37:2-6,16,23-24

Positional Symmetry
(Requisite Mirror Image)

The scientific community describes the origin of the universe in terms of the "Big Bang." The Big Bang is perhaps from a visual point of view somewhat descriptive of the beginning; as one may note viewing the **Alpha** pole.

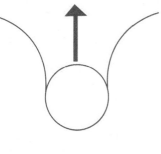

Science informs us that the Big Bang created the matter in the universe. The Big Bang, however, cannot explain the existence of space and time itself. The big bang? We need a more informative name for an event so meaningful as the origin of the universe.

Material reality is a tiny fraction of the observable universe. The scientists say that it is less than 4%. Most of the universe is space and time. It is either spacetime expanding (Dark Energy), or it is spacetime contracting (Dark Matter).

The contracting spacetime introduces acceleration and gravity, which is the beginning of some thing. The perspective over broad views reveals that the *cosmos is the context of existence*. The cosmos is, above all frames of references, an entity onto itself. The space and time of the cosmos, like water to the ocean, is invisible and everywhere. When we examine the properties of water, we observe not only that water is necessary for life, but there is an abundance of life in water, even at extreme conditions.

Matter, exist in space and time originating at the internal, most finite boundary of the universe, at the most finite scale. If the big bang occurred some 13.7 million years ago and it created the matter in the observable universe, what then provides the account for the space and time in which the 'now', is embedded to allow for the beginning of the universe? Where does the spacetime come from that inflates the universe for the matter to spread through? And what is the universe expanding into?

The event that scientists have termed the Big Bang marks the beginning of the universe of spacetime. The simplicity of my argument lies in the word, 'beginning.' It is the most accurate and informative description of the beginning; in fact it is spot on. The big bang is a misnomer because it is descriptive but not informative. In the beginning was the word, the "Beginning."

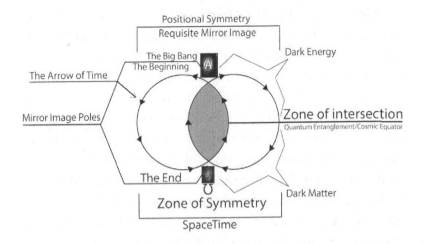

The relationship between the beginning event and the end, is not simply linear. The big bang event cannot precede the big crunch event as has been debated. This linear model of thinking suggests that the universe may collapse into nonexistence. Leading some to postulate a vacillating universe. This direction of thought is misleading.

The relationship between the beginning and the end, is that they exist *simultaneously* as mirror image poles. This means that conceptually, the ending should ideally be considered first because then the beginning, is implied existing automatically. The beginning is implied inherently and *simultaneously* because when you say the end, the end of what is implied and this in-turn refers back to its beginning.

"Remember the former things of old: For **I AM** God
and *there is none else;*
I AM God, and there is none like me.
Declaring the *end* from the *beginning,*
and from ancient times the things that are *not yet done;*
saying my counsel shall stand,

and I will do all my pleasure:"
Isaiah 46:9,10

Notice the wording here, "declaring the end from the beginning." The beginning therefore exist *implicitly* because the ending, in that it comes from its beginning, it is tied conceptually to the beginning; and cannot exist independent of its beginning. Your thinking must incorporate both poles simultaneously.

When the mirror image poles, which are 'probabilities,' intersect generating spontaneously, the zone of intersection: this domain has the property of *"instantaneous communications"* between the poles. The spontaneously generated domain in the *"intersection between the poles,"* is the fundamental cause that creates reality.

Any declaration of GOD is an existing thing because it is a wave emitted in the cosmic ocean. Alpha and Omega is an existing thing, it is an object we call, *'spacetime,'* which fills the void in the meaning from beginning to end.

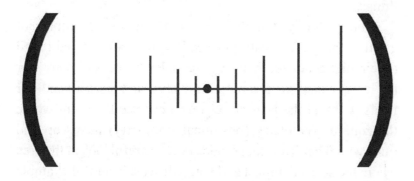

The ZOI is the key element in this dynamic process. For Western eyes, the ZOI serves as the source and meaning for the iconic fish symbol, known as the *ichthys*, that pervades Christianity. We see the Jesus-fish symbol on cars and it is generally used to identify people who call themselves Christians, but do you know what that symbol really means? Why was this symbol so important not just in early Christian art and architecture, but also in Freemasonry?

This symbol is very important, it is known as the *vesica pisces*[13]. The *vessica pisces* symbol serves as the basic symbol that describes the patterns formed by space as it expands. This concept is known as the flower of life in sacred geometry.

I am suggesting that if you take a careful look at the zone of intersection, you will see the source of the iconic 'fish' symbol of Christianity. But there is more here; the zone of intersection, or the *ichthys,* is a beautiful candidate for the 'inflaton'— which is "the field whose energy and negative pressure drives inflationary expansion."[14] This is the scientific community's proposed source for the inflationary expansion of the universe. Take a careful look at it and you will see how it pops!

If GOD is the creator of all things, then all things are formed in GOD's image. My intent now is to demonstrate how this proposed fundamental template is used to form all existing things.

The butterfly and the pear, are ordinary examples of existing things. You can now see how they are formed based on circuits generated between the poles 'mind and body' for the living conscious creatures, and 'stem and blossom end' for fruits. Look at the pear closely. You can see the seam where the zone of symmetry (positional symmetry) meets up and links with the mirror image side. Take a careful look at the area where the seeds manifest and you will see a beautiful example of the zone of intersection.

---

[13] https://en.wikipedia.org/wiki/Vesica_piscis
[14] Greene, B., *The Fabric of the Cosmos,* p539

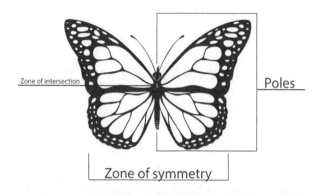

Zone of intersection

Poles

Zone of symmetry

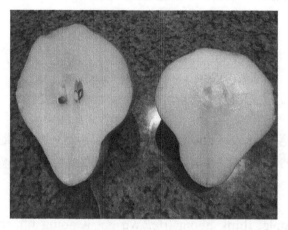

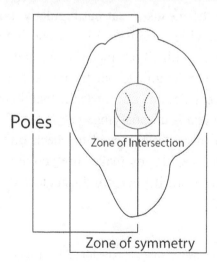

Poles

Zone of Intersection

Zone of symmetry

Thy Kingdom Come

"Now therefore thus saith the Lord of hosts;
consider your ways.
Ye have sown much, and bring in little;
ye eat, but ye have not enough;
ye drink, but ye are not filled with drink;
ye clothe you, but there is none warm;
and he that earneth wages
earneth wages to put it into a bag with holes.
Thus saith the Lord of hosts; *consider your ways.*"
Haggai 1:5-7

Hey people, think about life. We got it going on, that's for sure. We have the means to eat out regularly, go to bars and restaurants, enjoying ourselves. Life is one big commercial, friends. But, even with all our material needs met, we can see that there is never enough. Despite the denial of some amongst us, many of us can see and acknowledge that this way of life is not sustainable and is unsatisfying.

We are all aware of the need to check ourselves before we wreck ourselves. "If you make sure you're connected, the writing's on the wall, if your mind's neglected, you stumble you might fall."[15]

---

[15] lyrics from Stereo MC's song, "Somethin' Ain't Right." 1992

"And therefore will the Lord wait,
that he may be gracious unto you,
and therefore will he be exalted,
that he may have mercy upon you:
for the Lord is a God of judgment:
blessed are all they that
wait for him.
For the people shall dwell in Zion at Jerusalem:
Thou shalt weep no more:
he will be very gracious unto thee
at the voice of thy cry;
when he shall hear it, he will answer thee.
And though the Lord give you
the bread of adversity,
and the water of affliction,
**yet shall not thy teachers be
removed into a corner any more,
but thine eyes shall see thy teachers:**
And thine ears shall hear a word behind thee, saying,
this is the way, walk ye in it,"
Isaiah 30: 18-21

There is a lot going on here in this wonderful scripture. It explains that GOD is waiting for the ideal time in human history to seamlessly pull of the plan. GOD wants the work done in such a way as to deny the antichrists the power to kill his messengers. GOD acknowledges that we the people, have suffered much in the meantime.

"He that hath an ear,
let him hear what the *Spirit* saith unto the churches;
to him that overcometh will I give to eat of the

tree of life,
which is in the midst of the *paradise of God.*
...He that overcometh shall not be
hurt of the second death.
...To him that overcometh will I give to eat of the
hidden manna ["mindstuff"], and
will give him a white stone,
and in the stone, a new name written
which no man knoweth saving he that receiveth it.
...He that overcometh,
the same shall be clothed in white raiment;
and I will not blot out his name out of the book of life,
but I will confess his name before my Father,
and before his angels...
Him that overcometh will I make a pillar
in the temple of my GOD
...and I will write upon him *my new name."*
Revelation 2:7,11,17

"Behold, I stand at the door, and knock:
if any man here my voice, and open the door,
I will come in to him, and will sup
with him, and he with me.
To him that overcometh will I grant
to sit with me in my throne,
even as I also overcame, and am set down
with my Father *in his throne.*
He that hath an ear, let him hear what the *Spirit*
saith unto the churches."
Revelation 3:5,12,20-22

"I AM the Lord thy GOD,
which brought thee out of the land of the Egypt:
open thy mouth wide and I will fill it.
But my people would not hearken to my voice;
and Israel would none of me."
Psalm 81:10,11

"Thus saith the Lord concerning the prophets
that make my people to err,
that bite with their teeth, and cry, peace;
and *he that putteth not into their mouths...*"
Micah 3:5

"Thy words were found, and *I did eat them;*
and thy word was unto me
the joy and rejoicing of mine heart:
for I am called by thy name, O Lord GOD of hosts."
Jeremiah 15:16

"And thou shalt speak unto him,
and *put words in his mouth:*
and I will be with thy mouth, and with his mouth,
and will teach you what ye shall do."
Exodus 4:15

"Behold, the days come, saith the Lord,
that I will make a *new covenant*
with the house of Israel and with the house of **Judah:**
Not according to the covenant that I made
with their fathers in the day that
I took them by the hand

72

to lead them out of the land of Egypt...
But this shall be the covenant that I will make
with the house of Israel;
after those days...
I will put my law in their inward parts
and write it in their hearts;
and will be their God,
and they shall be my people:"
Hebrews 8:8-10 & Jeremiah 31:31-33.

"And I will give them one heart, and *one way*,
that they may fear me forever, for the good of them,
and of their children after them:
And I will make an *everlasting covenant* with them,
that *I will not turn away from*
them, to do them good;
but I will put my fear in their hearts,
that they shall not depart from me.
...Behold, **I AM** the Lord, The God of all flesh:
is there anything too hard for me?
Jeremiah 32:39-40,27

"And they shall teach no more every man his neighbor,
and every man his brother, saying,
know the Lord: *for they shall all know me*,
from the least of them unto the
greatest of them, saith the Lord:
for I will forgive their iniquity,
and I will remember their sin no more."
Jeremiah 31:34

I understand that it is very important to make certain that Jeremiah's vision here is very clear. The word says that there will come a time when there are no longer televangelists and preachers everywhere saying, "come here, so that you can learn about God." There is no need to inform anyone because everyone will know God.

"Thou shalt not see a fierce people,
a people of a *deeper speech* than thou canst perceive;
of a stammering tongue, that thou
canst not understand."
Isaiah 33:19

"Thus saith the **LORD** the **KING** of Israel,
and his redeemer the LORD of hosts;
I AM the first, and **I AM** the last;
And beside me there is no GOD."
Isaiah 44:6

How
To
Come
Back
To
The
Remembrance
Of
God
Through

"I sought in mine heart to give myself unto wine,
yet acquainting mine heart with wisdom;
and to lay hold on folly, till I might see
what was that good for the sons of men,
which they should do under the heaven
all the days of their life."

Ecclesiastes 2:3

There is an ongoing and continuous discussion in societies everywhere about ideas thought to help us in life. You know, take your vitamins, laws against bad behaviors, ways to improve health, daily talk shows, etc.

In the United States, we have one of the most advanced healthcare systems in the world, yet we expect that if we should live a long life, we can expect to live into our mid-70's or so.

Given our short lifespans, the question remains, "what was that good thing that we need to do as living conscious beings, that allows us to live on and create a glorious future for all?"

"Thus saith the Lord, stand ye in the ways, and see,
and ask for the old paths,
where is the good way, and walk therein,
and ye shall find rest for you souls.
But they said, we will not walk therein."

Jeremiah 6:16

"The secret things belong unto the Lord our God:
but those things which are *revealed*
belong unto us and to our children forever,
that we may do all the words of this law."

Deuteronomy 29:29

"For when for the time ye ought to be teachers,
you have need that one teach you *again*
which be the first principles of
the *Oracles* of *God,*"
Hebrews 5:12

The first principle of the oracles of God is that the 'I' must *meditate*. This is spiritual law necessitated by the *Fall*. The 'fall' refers to the force of gravity in galaxies as time moves towards the end.

The lifespans of living material creatures are short because of the literal distance between infinity and any given being that comes into existence in the here and now. The "here and now" is so finite, it is a categorical designation that means that we are existentially estranged from GOD whom we can never reach, because we are so finite; whereas GOD is everywhere, conscious, and everlasting.

The literal experience of our limited finite consciousness is that our thoughts become estranged from higher order holistic thoughts as we create constricted linear ways of thinking consistent with the *gravity* of the situation. This is corruption, when the only choices we can conceive are the best of two evils. We then believe and follow our own thoughts.

These are the types of thoughts that emerge when born in the context of the spiraling galactic swirl; toward the end. The Earth's position for example, is some 25,000 light years from the supermassive black hole in the center of our galaxy. According to science, there are about a million times more dark matter here in the galaxy than at the periphery of the galaxy.

The black hole is an agent of the universe; it is the end. The end, however, must have an ending derived from the spacetime from the beginning. So the ending is the part of the story that comes from the beginning, but now we are near the end of the story, the part that leads directly to the end.

Galaxies are routinely about one hundred thousand light years across and bigger; and they increase in size orders of magnitudes of scale. The average depth of the Milky Way, for example, is about 10,000 light years and it increases to about 30,000 light years toward the center.[16]

The amazing thing about galaxies is that you can see plainly that the arrow of time is moving toward the black hole from either side of the galaxy. There is no front and back of the galaxy. It's a one-way road to oblivion whether you are one side of the universe moving toward the end, or the other side moving toward the end. All lines are leading to one place, *on either side*; so as you approach the galactic center, *the universe is behind you.*

This explains how we are literally estranged from God. Material beings are born in the context of the ending—the bent spacetime of the galaxy. Time, at this place, is moving relentlessly, like a waterfall, toward the black hole. The fountain of life, which is dark energy, is the dominant feature of the universe, yet it is far removed from us; or rather, we are far removed from it. Gravity is the boss in the here and now, and thus we must all deal with the grave, which is the end.

The stories of humans and their developments of societies, betrays a grotesque divide between our hopes and aspirations as sentient beings of the cosmos, and our behaviors. Yet, we cannot separate our behaviors from our thought-lives. As people think in their hearts, so are we in our lives. We are responsible for not only our thoughts but also our behaviors. The fundamental problem lies in that our thought-lives have changed awry

---

[16] http://www.infoplease.com/encyclopedia/science/milky-way-size-shape-milky-way.html

from higher order (*spirit/celestial*) thoughts to focused, linear, polarizing, thoughts based on an agenda, because of lack.

The way of this path has accelerated knowledge of good, and *evil* but the consciousness of "freespace celestial" with its hidden internal and external dimensions, *"simultaneity"* events on manifold levels; are unknown. **We must be born again**. We must come again to a new beginning. The beginning is what we are all seeking to evolve to a higher sentience.

The law of the fall is inherent within the context of the galaxy system; this is what our scientist call dark matter. Human thoughts must transcend the depths against the gravity of the spiraling galaxy system, to enter freespace, which has many many mansions. One must therefore ***meditate*** by intoning the word, '**I AM**,' in whatever language you speak.

One must intone the name '**I AM**' to counteract the fall. It is understood that this law of oral meditations is referred to in the bible in the meaning in the word, 'testimony.' One, who meditates in the testimony of God, is in *covenant* with God. The recitation of these meditations transforms minds to a spirit obedient, enabling humanity the 'state of mind' to fulfill the written law. Which is to say that human behavior improves.

"As for me, this is my *covenant* with them,
saith the Lord; My spirit that is upon thee,
and my *words* which I have put in thy *mouth*,..."
Isaiah 59:21

"And he brought forth the king's son,
and put the crown upon him,
and gave him the *testimony*;
and they made him king and anointed him;
and they clapped their hands, and said,

God save the king."
11 Kings 11:12

"I am thy fellowservant, and of thy brethren that have
the testimony of Jesus: worship God;
for the testimony of Jesus is the spirit of prophecy."
Revelation 19:10

The words, "the testimony of Jesus is the spirit of prophecy,"
reveals that these spoken words of meditations, i.e., the testimony,
is spirit. The meaning in and of the meditations, manifest itself
as a spirit or way of consciousness in the community of those
who maintain the meditations daily. The agreement or covenant
lies in the contract that both elements are necessary together.
We have to meditate, and the spirit will manifest.

"And Isaac went out to meditate
in the field as eventide."
Genesis 24:63

Indeed the words of the oral covenant, or testimony, were
long neglected and forgotten by the religious leaders; leading
them astray, though many were sincerely engaged in ceremony
and reading the scriptures.

We see clearly today that the religious leaders and their
followers do not reflect the spirit and love of Christ. They
subscribed to GOD's word and took it upon themselves to teach
the people, however, they neglected the oral part of the law, so
they became ravenous wolves in sheep's clothing.

"Therefore have I also made you contemptible
and base before all the people,
according as ye have not kept my ways,

but have been partial in the law."
Malachi 2:9

"But unto the wicked God saith,
what hast thou to do to declare my statutes,
or that thou shouldest take
my *covenant in thy mouth*?"
Seeing thou hatest instruction,
and castest my *words* behind thee,"
Psalm 50:16,17

"Whoso despiseth the word shall be destroyed:
but he that feareth the commandment will be rewarded.
The law of the wise is a fountain of life,
To deliver from the snares of death."
Proverb 13:13,14

"...his delight is in the law of the Lord;
and in his law doth he *meditate day* and night.
And he shall be like a tree planted by the rivers of water,
that bringeth forth his fruit in his season;
his leaf also shall not wither;
and whatsoever he doeth shall prosper."
Psalm 1:2,3

"He that believeth on me, as the scripture hath said,
out of his belly shall flow *rivers of living water.*"
John 7:38

In the patriarchal societies of our past, to speak of the male
would automatically imply the female. The male child is born
from the mother. There is no implicit neglect. There is explicit

neglect, perceived from the perspective of modern day society, and in history. My explicit apologies to our daughters and sisters, wives and mothers, aunts and nieces.

"...whosoever drinketh of the water that I shall give him shall never thirst; but the water that I shall give him shall be in him a well of water
springing up into everlasting life."
John 4:14

"...Christ is the head of the church:
and he is the saviour of the body.
...Christ also loved the church, and gave himself for it;
that he might sanctify and cleanse it
with the *washing of the water*
by the word.
That he might present to himself a glorious church,
Not having spot or wrinkle, or any such thing;
but that it should be holy and without blemish."
Ephesians 5:23,25-27

"And they overcame him by the blood of the lamb,
and by the *word* of their *testimony;*
and they loved not their lives unto the death."
Revelation 12:11

We have here, the definition of the church that is the true church of GOD and not a church of human religion. The scriptures disclose that there are three elements defining the church: the saints overcome the power of the fall by the power of the blood of the lamb, they meditate daily, and they live on, they do not die.

This is the secret in the mystery of Jesus' death. He was manifested as a human yet with a consciousness of GOD. With his sacrificial death, he can now bridge the gap between the finite and infinity. That is why the story of his death includes a resurrection and ascension. Remember, our job is to meditate daily.

"The law of the Lord is perfect, *converting the soul:*
the *testimony* of the Lord is sure,
making wise the simple."
Psalm 19:7

"I am thy servant; give me understanding,
that I may know thy *testimonies.*
Thy *testimonies* are wonderful:
therefore doth my soul keep them.
The entrance of thy words giveth light;
it giveth understanding unto the simple."
Psalm 119:125,129-130

"Blessed are they that keep his *testimonies*
and that seek him with the whole heart.
They also do no iniquity:
they walk in his ways.
Thou hast commanded us to
keep thy precepts diligently."
Psalm 119: 2-4

"I have more understanding than all my teachers:
for thy testimonies are my meditation.
Oh how I love thy law! It is my meditation
all the day."
Psalm 119:99,97

"If thy children will keep my **covenant** and
my **testimony** *that I shall teach them,*
their children also shall sit upon
thy throne for evermore."
Psalm 132:12

"Incline my heart unto thy **testimonies,**
and not to covetousness.
So shall I keep thy law continually forever and ever.
And I will walk at liberty: for I seek thy precepts.
I will speak of thy **testimonies** also before kings,
and will not be ashamed."
Psalm 119:36,44-46

"And they that shall be of thee shall
build the old waste places:
thou shalt raise up the foundation of many generations;
and thou shalt be called,
the **repairer of the breach,**
the restorer of paths to dwell in."
Isaiah 58:11-12

*"And I will bring the blind by a way
that they knew not;*
I will lead them in paths that they have not known:
I will make darkness light before them,
and crooked things straight.
These things will I do unto them,
and not forsake them.
...Hear ye deaf; and look, ye blind, that ye may see...
But this is a people robbed and spoiled;
they are all of them snared in holes,

and **they are hid in prison houses:**
they are for a prey, and none delivereth;
for a spoil, and none saith, Restore."
Isaiah 42:16,18,22

I think again that it is important to note here that God speaks about his people as being exploited and imprisoned.

"Behold, I will do a new thing;
now it shall spring forth;
shall ye not know it?
I will even make a way in the wilderness,
and rivers in the dessert...
This people have I formed for myself;
they shall show forth my praise."
Isaiah 43:19,21

"Turn you at my reproof:
behold, I will pour out my *spirit* unto you,
I will make known my *words* unto you."
Proverbs 1:23

"In the morning *sow thy seed*, and in the evening
withhold not thine hand:
For thou knowest not whether shall prosper,
either this or that,
or whether they both be alike good.

We do not know what will prosper. Either this or that, or perhaps both are alike equally good

Let us hear the conclusion of the whole matter:
Fear God, and keep his commandments:
for this is the whole duty of man.
For God shall bring every work into judgment,
with every secret thing,
whether it be good, or whether it be evil."
Ecclesiastes 11:6 & 12:13-14

"Wherefore then serveth the Law?
It was added because of transgressions,
till the seed should come to whom
the promise was made;
and it was ordained by angels in
the hand of a *mediator*."
Galatians 3:19

"Whosoever is born of God doth not commit sin;
for his **seed** remaineth in him:
and he cannot sin, because he is born of God.
In this the children of God are manifest,
and the children of the devil:
whosoever doeth not righteousness is not of God,
neither he that loveth not his brother."
1 John 3:9,10

"For whatsoever is born of GOD overcometh the world...
We know that whosoever is born of GOD sinneth not;
but he that is begotten of GOD keepeth himself,
...little children keep yourselves from idols. Amen."
1 John 5:4,18,21

I AM one with JESUS THE MESSIAH
I AM one with Space eternal, everlasting
I AM one with Time eternal, everlasting
I AM one with the HOLY SPIRIT

I AM a smooth, agile, eloquent swimmer
in the sea (reality)

I AM the salt of the earth
I AM wisdom and understanding

I hold and direct the bridle reality
I AM one with JESUS THE MESSIAH
I AM one with the HOLY SPIRIT

I achieve in leaps and bounds.
I AM power, beauty, in JESUS THE MESSIAH
I visualize vividly

Father I AM in thine thoughts, in accord...
in thine thoughts

I AM a successfully influential child of I AM
for ever and ever

Recite these meditations at least 7 times each, over and over every morning as you arise, and at night before sleep. Recite during the day and again at night, everyday.

"This is the bread which cometh down from heaven,
that a man may eat thereof, *and not die.*
I AM the living bread which came down from heaven:
If any man eat of this bread he shall live forever..."
John 6:50-51

"This is the rest wherewith ye may
cause the weary to rest;
and this is the refreshing..."
Isaiah 28:12

"Another parable put he forth unto them, saying,
the kingdom of heaven is likened unto a man
which sowed good *seed* in his field..."
Matthew 13:24

"Verily, verily, I say unto thee,
except a man be *born again*,
he cannot see the kingdom of God.
...except a man be born of the
water and of the *Spirit*
he cannot enter into the kingdom of God."
John 3:3,5

"Now the parable is this:
the seed is the word of God."
Luke 8:11

The cosmos is composed of spacetime. The cosmic ocean
is the fundamental frame of reference within which events
originate and play out. The *water* is therefore necessary for life
and expression. The spoken word is *spirit* because as a wave in

88

the ocean, it is a transmission through spacetime of form and meaning.

The oral law is to meditate using spoken words and their implicit meanings, to elicit fundamental states of consciousness consistent with universal protocol. The meaning fills the mind like dark energy in the cosmos.

"I beseech you therefore, brethren,
by the mercies of God,
that ye present your bodies a living sacrifice,
holy, acceptable to God,
which is your reasonable service,
and be not conformed to this world:
but be ye transformed by the
renewing of your mind,
that ye may prove what is that good, and acceptable,
and perfect will of God."
Romans 12:1,2

We see here that the interplay between the poles 'mind and body' creates the soul–a singular being. I suppose that 'mind and body' are the mirror image poles that create living biological beings. We see plainly here that the salvation of the soul is in the mind, to save the body.

"There are also celestial bodies, and bodies terrestrial:
but the glory of the celestial is one,
and the glory of the terrestrial is another.
It is sown a natural body; it is raised a spiritual body.
There is a natural body, and *there is a spiritual body.*
The first man is of the earth, earthy:
the second man is the Lord from heaven."
1 Corinthians 15:40,44,47

"And as we have born the image of the earthy,
we shall also bear the image of the heavenly.
Now this I say, brethren, that *flesh and blood*
cannot inherit the kingdom of God;
neither doth corruption inherit incorruption.
For this corruptible must put on incorruption,
And this mortal must put on immortality."
1 Corinthians 15:49,50,53

"That which is born of flesh is flesh;
and that which is born of Spirit is spirit.
Marvel not that I said unto thee,
ye must be born again."
John 3:6,7

We must undergo evolutionary growth to a new stage in our development.

"They which are the children of the flesh,
these are not the children of God:
but the children of the promise are counted
for the *seed. For this is the word of promise,*
at this time will I come..."
Romans 9:8,9

"As long as **I AM** in the world,
I AM the light of the world."
John 9:5

"But this I say, he which soweth sparingly
shall reap also sparingly;
and he which soweth bountifully

shall reap also bountifully."
2 Corinthians 9:6

"Jesus answered and said unto him,
if a man love me, he will keep my words:
and my Father will love him,
and we will come unto him, and
make our abode with him.
He that loveth me not keepeth not my sayings..."
John 14:23-24

"...when thou shalt make his soul an offering for sin,
he shall see his *seed*,
he shall prolong his days,
and the pleasure of the Lord shall prosper in his hand."
Isaiah 53:10

"If ye continue in my word, then
are ye my disciples indeed;
and ye shall know the truth,
and the truth shall make you free."
John 8:31-32

"Verily, verily, I say unto you if a man keep my saying,
he shall never see death."
John 8:51

"And I have put my words *in thy mouth*,
and I have covered thee in the shadow of mine hand,
that I may plant the heavens,
and lay the foundations of the earth,
and say unto Zion, thou art my people."
Isaiah 51:16

"And these words, which I command thee this day,
shall be in thine heart:
and thou shalt teach them diligently unto thy children,
and thou shalt talk of them when
thou sittest in thine house,
and when thou walkest by the way,
and when thou **liest down,** and when thou **risest up.**
...and they shall be as frontlets between thine eyes."

Deuteronomy 6:6-8

"For he established a **testimony** in Jacob,
and appointed a **law** in Israel,
which he commanded our fathers,
that they should *make them known to their children*:
...yet they tempted and provoked the most high GOD,
and kept not his **testimonies:"**

Psalm 78:5,56

"Thus saith the Lord,
as the *new wine* is found in the cluster,
and **one** saith, destroy it not;
for a blessing is in it:
so will I do for my servants' sakes,
that I may not destroy them all.
And I will bring forth a seed out of Jacob,
and out of Judah **an inheritor of my mountains:**
and mine elect shall inherit it,
and my servants shall dwell there...
For, behold, I create **new heavens and a new earth:**
and the former shall not be remembered,
nor come to mind...
There shall be no more thence an infant of days,

nor an old man that hath not filled his days:
for the child shall die an hundred years old;
but the sinner being an hundred
years old shall be accursed.
**...for as the days of a tree are
the days of my people,**
and mine elect shall long enjoy the work of their hands.
They shall not labour in vain, nor bring forth trouble;
for they are the *seed* of the blessed of the Lord,
and their offspring with them.
And it shall come to pass, that before they call,
I will answer;
and while they are yet speaking,
I will hear.
The wolf and the lamb shall feed together,
and the lion shall eat straw like the bullock:
and dust shall be the serpent's meat.
They shall not hurt nor destroy in all my holy mountain,
saith the Lord."
Isaiah 65:8,9,17,20,22-25

The vision of reality described in this text refers to a time when humanity has evolved to an entirely different scale in consciousness relative to the 'dog-eat-dog' way of life on Earth in the past. It begins with a warning describing the fact that we are essentially on the edge between extinction and eternal life. During this period of transition, if you remain in a corrupted state, you will die, even if you live to be one hundred years old.

God promises that he will be attentive to intervene to save the ones he has chosen to live. The lifespan for the *millennial elect* is very different to the extent that if you live to be one hundred years old, you are actually only a child. This means that the scale of our existence will change from the finite moving toward the infinite.

The people who experience this reality will live very long extended lives characterized by a closeness to the divine, to the extent that our communion is so intimate that answers to our questions and requests of God will often come *while we are making the requests.* Whaaat! GOD is in disguise as Amazon's delivery?

It appears that the times will be so peaceful, and the Earth so productive in terms of the ecology of the land, that we will move increasingly towards sustained vegetarian diets of vast diversity, eating sunlight indirectly, and no one will seek to bring harm to any living creature for any reason because, all of our needs will be satisfied in a society driven by GOD consciousness.

"And strangers shall stand and feed your flocks,
and the sons of the alien shall be your plowmen
and your vinedressers.
But ye shall be named the *Priest of the Lord:*
men shall call you the *Ministers of our God:*
ye shall eat the riches of the Gentiles,
and in their glory shall ye boast yourselves.
For your shame ye shall have double;
...they shall possess the double:
everlasting joy shall be unto them.
...I will direct their work in truth,
and I will make an everlasting covenant with them.
And their seed shall be among the Gentiles,
and their offspring among the people:
all that see them shall acknowledge them,
that they are the *seed*

which the Lord hath blessed...
For as the earth bringeth forth her bud,
and as the garden causeth the things
that are *sown* in it to spring forth;
so the Lord GOD will cause righteousness
and praise to spring forth
before all the nations."
Isaiah 61:5-9,11

"For thus saith the Lord,
behold I will extend peace to her like a river,
and the glory of the Gentiles like a flowing stream:
then shall ye suck, ye shall be borne upon her sides,
and be dandled upon her knees.
As one whom his mother comforteth,
so will I comfort you;
and ye shall be comforted in Jerusalem.
And when ye see this, your heart shall rejoice,
and your bones shall flourish like an herb:
and the hand of the Lord shall be known towards
his servants,
and his indignation toward his enemies.
For, behold, the Lord will come with fire,
and with his chariots like a whirlwind,
to render his anger with fury,
and his rebuke with *flames of fire.*
For by fire and by his sword
will the Lord plead with all flesh:
and the slain of the Lord shall be many.
...and it shall come,
that I will gather all nations and tongues;
and they shall come, and *see my glory."*

For as the new heavens and the new earth,
which I will make,
shall remain before me, saith the Lord,
so shall your seed and your name remain.
And it shall come to pass, that from one new moon
to another, and from one sabbath to another,
shall all flesh come to worship before me..."
Isaiah 66:12-16,18,22,23

"Behold, the Lord hath a mighty and strong one,
which as a **tempest of hail** and a
destroying storm,
as a flood of mighty waters overflowing,
shall cast down to the earth with the hand...
Whom shall he teach knowledge?
And whom shall he make to understand doctrine...
For precept must be upon precept,
precept upon precept;
line upon line, line upon line;
here a little, and there a little:"
Isaiah 28:2,9,10

"If any man serve me, let him follow me;
and where **I AM,**
there shall also my servant be:
if any man serve me, him will my **Father** honour...
Father, glorify thy name.
Then came there a voice from heaven, saying,
I have both glorified it, and will glorify it again."
John 12:26,28

"And it shall come to pass in that day,

96

that the Lord shall set his hand **again**
the second time
to recover the remnant of his people...
And in that day shall ye say, praise the Lord,
call upon his name,
declare his doings among the people,
make mention that his name is exalted.
...for great is the Holy One of Israel
in the midst of thee."
Isaiah 11:11 & 12:4

"The Kingdom of God cometh *not with observation:*
neither shall they say, lo here, or, lo there.
For behold, the Kingdom of God is **within you."**
Luke 17:20,21

"And the Lord God of their fathers sent to them
by his messengers; rising betimes, and sending;
because he had compassion on his people,
and on his dwelling place:
but they mocked the messengers of God,
and despised his words, and misused his prophets,
until the wrath of the Lord arose against his people,
till there was no remedy."
2 Chronicles 36:15,16

"O Israel return unto the Lord thy GOD;
for thou hast fallen by thine iniquity.
Take with you words, and turn to the Lord:
say unto him, take away all iniquity,
and receive us graciously...
...neither will we say any more to the work of our hands,

Ye are our Gods; for in thee the fatherless find mercy.
I will heal their backsliding, I will love them freely.
For mine anger is turned away from him."

Hosea 14:1-4

"All the paths of the Lord are mercy
and truth unto such as
keep his **covenant** and his **testimonies.**"

Psalm 25:10

Bind up the **testimony,**
seal the **law** among my disciples...
To the **law** and to the **testimony;**
If they speak not according to this word,
it is because there is no light in them.
And they shall pass thru it hardly bestead and hungry:
[famine?]
and it shall come to pass, that when
they shall be hungry, they shall fret themselves,
and curse their king and their God, and look upward.
And they shall look unto the earth;
and *behold trouble and darkness,*
dimness of anguish;
and they shall be driven to darkness."

Isaiah 8:16,20-22

Therefore thus saith the Lord GOD,
Behold, my servants shall eat,
but ye shall be hungry:
behold, my servants shall drink,
but ye shall be thirsty:
behold, my servants shall sing for joy of heart,

but ye shall cry for sorrow of heart, and shall howl
for vexation of spirit.

Isaiah 65: 13-14

"I will declare thy name unto my brethren:
in the midst of the congregation will I praise thee.
Ye that fear the Lord, praise him; all ye seed of Jacob,
glorify him; and fear him:
all ye seed of Israel.
For he hath not despised nor abhorred the affliction of
the afflicted; neither hath he hid his face from him;
but when he cried unto him, he heard...
The meek shall eat and be satisfied:
they shall praise the Lord that seek him:
your heart shall live for ever.
**All the ends of the world shall remember
and turn unto the Lord:
and all the kindreds of the nations
shall worship before thee.**
For the kingdom is the Lord's:
and he is the governor among the nations.
All they that be fat upon the earth shall eat and worship:
all they that go down to the dust shall bow before him:
and *none can keep alive his own soul.*
**A seed shall serve him;
it shall be accounted to the Lord for a generation.**
They shall come,..."

Psalm 22:22-24,26-31

"When the Lord turned again the captivity of Zion,
we were like them that dream.
Then was our mouth filled with laughter,

and our tongue with singing:
then said they among the heathen,
the Lord hath done great things for them.
The Lord hath done great things for us;
whereof we are glad.
Turn again our captivity, O Lord,
as the streams in the south.
They that sow in tears shall reap in joy.
He that goeth forth and weepeth,
bearing **precious seed,**
shall doubtless come again with rejoicing,
bringing his sheaves with him."

Psalm 126

"For every man shall bear his own burden.
Let him that is taught in the word
communicate unto him that teacheth in all good things.
Be not deceived; God is not mocked.
For *whatsoever a man soweth,* that shall he also reap,
...he that soweth to the *Spirit* shall of the *Spirit*
reap life everlasting."

Galatians 6:5-8

"I AM ALPHA AND OMEGA,
the beginning and the end, the first and the last.
Blessed are they that do his commandments,
that they may have right to the *tree of life,*
and may enter in through the gates into the city.
For without are dogs, and sorcerers, and whoremongers,
and murderers, and idolaters,
and whosoever loveth and maketh a lie.

I **JESUS** have sent mine angel
[messenger] to testify unto you
these things in the churches.
I am the root and the offspring of David,
and the bright and morning star.
And the *Spirit* and the bride say, come.
And let him that heareth say, come.
And let him that is athirst come.
And whosoever will,
let him take of the *water of life* freely."

Revelations 22:13-17

"Thus saith the Lord;
if ye can break my **covenant** of the day,
and my **covenant** of the night,
and that there should not be *day* and **night**
in their season;
Then may also my **covenant** be broken with David
my servant, that he should not have a son to
reign upon his throne; ...Thus saith the Lord;
if my **covenant be not with day and night,**
*and if I have not appointed the ordinances of
heaven and earth;*
Then will I cast away the seed of Jacob,
and David my servant,
so that I will not take any of his seed to be rulers
over the seed of Abraham, Isaac, and Jacob:
For I will cause their captivity to return,
an have mercy on them."

Jeremiah 33:20-21,25-26

"Hearken unto me, O Jacob and Israel, my called;
I AM he;
I AM the first, I also **AM** the last.
Mine hand also hath laid the foundations of the earth,
and my right hand hath spanned the heavens:
when I call unto them *they stand up together..*
Thus saith the Lord, thy Redeemer,
the Holy One of Israel;
I AM the Lord thy GOD which teacheth thee to profit,
which leadeth thee by the way that thou shouldest go.
O that thou hadst hearkened to my commandments!
Then had thine peace been as a river,
and thy righteousness as *the waves of the sea.*"
Isaiah 48:12,13,17

"**I AM** the Lord, and *there is none else,*
there is no God beside me:
I girded thee, *though thou hast not known me:*
That they may know from the rising of the sun,
and from the west, that there is none beside me.
I AM the Lord, *and there is none else.*
I form the light, and create darkness.

I make peace and create evil:
I the Lord do all these things...
For thus saith the Lord that created the heavens;
God himself that formed the earth and made it;
he hath established it, he created it not in vain,
he formed it to be inhabited:
I AM the Lord, and *there is none else.*
...there is no God else beside me;
a just God and a saviour;
there is none beside me.
Look unto me, and be ye saved,
all the ends of the earth;
for **I AM GOD**, *and there is none else.*
I have sworn by myself, the word
is gone out of my mouth
in righteousness and shall not return,
that unto me every knee shall bow,
and every tongue shall swear.
Surely, shall one say, in the Lord have I righteousness
and strength: even to him shall men come;
and all that are incensed against him
shall be ashamed.
In the Lord shall all the seed of Israel
be justified, and shall glory."
Isaiah 45:5-7,18,21-25

"For all people will walk *every one*
in the name of his God,
and we will walk **in the name of the Lord our GOD**
for ever and ever.
...and the Lord shall reign over them in mount Zion from
henceforth, even for ever...

Arise and thresh, O daughter of Zion:
for I will make thine horn iron,
and I will make thy hoofs brass:
and thou shalt beat in pieces many people:
and I will consecrate their gain unto the Lord,
and their substance unto the Lord of the whole earth."

Micah 4:5,7,13

"For whosoever shall call upon the name
of the Lord shall be saved."

Romans 10:13

"GOD is jealous, and the Lord **revengeth;**
the Lord **revengeth,** and is **furious;**
the Lord will take **vengeance** on his **adversaries,**
and he reserveth **wrath** for his **enemies.**
The Lord is slow to anger, and great in power,
and will not at all acquit the wicked:
the Lord hath his way in the whirlwind and in the storm,
and the clouds are the dust of his feet...
The mountains quake at him, and the hills melt,
and the earth is burned at his presence,
Yea, the world, and all that dwell therein.
Who can stand before his indignation?
And who can abide in the fierceness of his anger?
His fury is poured out like fire,
and the rocks are thrown down by him.
The Lord is good, a strong hold in the day of trouble;
and *he knoweth them that trust in him.*
But with and overrunning flood he will make
an utter end of the place thereof,
and darkness shall pursue his enemies.

...Though I have afflicted thee, I
will afflict thee no more.
For now will I break *his* yoke from off thee,
and will *burst thy bonds in sunder...*
Behold upon the mountains the feet of him that bringeth
good tidings, that publisheth peace!
O Judah, keep thy solemn feast, *perform thy vows:*
**For the wicked shall no more pass through thee;
he is utterly cut off."**
Nahum 1:2,3,5-8,12,13,15

"In that day will I make the governors of **judah**
like an **hearth of fire** among the wood,
and like a torch of fire in a sheaf;
and they shall devour all the people round about,
on the right hand and on the left:
and **Jerusalem shall be inhabited** *again*
in her own place, even in Jerusalem.
The Lord also shall save the tents of **Judah** *first,*
that the glory of the house of David
and the glory of the inhabitants of Jerusalem
do not magnify themselves against Judah.
In that day shall the Lord defend
the inhabitants of Jerusalem;
and he that is feeble among them at that day
shall be as David;
and the **house of David shall be as God,**
as the angel of the Lord before them.
And it shall come to pass in that day,
that I will seek to destroy all nations that
come against Jerusalem.
And I will pour upon the house of David,

and upon the inhabitants of Jerusalem,
the spirit of grace and supplications:
and they shall look upon me
whom they have pierced,
and they shall mourn for him,
as one mourneth for his only son,
and shall be in bitterness for him,
as one that is in bitterness for his **firstborn**."
Zechariah 12:6-10

The imagery evoked by Zechariah speaks directly to the ultimate redemption of Israel in terms of its, shall we say complicated, reconciliation with Jesus the messiah; "and they shall look upon me whom they had pierced...and mourn...as one that is in bitterness for his firstborn." We know that Israel rejected Jesus and to this day they are waiting on the messiah.

We know and acknowledge that Israel had twelve tribes. Jesus has been customarily described as the lion of the tribe of Judah. Judah, you may recall, was the fourth son of Jacob and fathered one of the twelve tribes of Israel, along with his brethren. Judah had married a woman of the Canaanites.[17] Canaan is a descendant of Ham, who is one of the sons of Noah.

According to the Hebrew tradition, the three sons of Noah who descended from the ark after the great deluge, fathered the three most general races of humans: namely, the Asian, the Negro, and the Caucasian.

Shem was the eldest son and in my opinion, represents Asiatic people in a very general sense. Shem is the root of the word 'semitic.' We think of Jewish people and the Arabs to be Semitic.

---

[17] Genesis chap. 38

Ham, it is noted, is the father of Canaan, Egypt, Ethiopia, and Phut (which some think to be Libya today). According to this tradition, Canaan was cursed to be the servant of his brethren because he had seen the nakedness of his father, Noah, which purportedly brought shame upon him.

Alternatively, Ham's name was added to Avram's, by God, forming the name Abraham. God then is noted to say to Abraham that he will be a father of many nations.

Japheth, according to Genesis 9:27, lived in the tents of Shem, his territory was to be extended, and Canaan was deemed to be his slave.

In my mind, Japheth represents the Europeans who are called Caucasians—indicating that they subsumed under the Asian identity. This in turn refers back to the idea of Japheth living in the tents of Shem. Certainly, the Europeans did extend their boundaries beyond Europe.

We understand that Noah was a direct descendent of Adam and retained his genetic legacy. The name Adam means "red man" and refers to the red dirt, perhaps much like our own Georgia clay here in America, from which he was formed.

In African American culture, we call people who are mixed-race, such as the mulatto, we call them 'red.' This is a common nickname in African-American communities. I understand that regardless of this idiomatic term, if all the races came from one genetic pool that branched early in its evolution to form the three races of humans, then the first humans contained in their genetic stock all information from the three races combined. They were mixed-race. They were mulatto, or 'redman.'

The Parable Of The Sower

"The same day went Jesus out of the house,
and sat by the sea side.
And great multitudes were gathered together unto him,
so that he went into a ship, and sat;
and the whole multitude stood on the shore.
And he spake many things unto
them in parables, saying,
Behold, a *sower* went forth to sow;
and when he sowed,
some *seeds* fell by the way side,
...some fell upon stony places,
...some fell among thorns..
But other fell into good ground,
and brought forth fruit, some an hundredfold,
some sixtyfold, some an thirtyfold.
Who hath ears to hear let him hear...
For whosoever hath [presumably of these seeds],
to him shall be given,
and he shall have more abundance:
but *whosoever hath not*,
from him shall be taken away even that he hath.

Hear ye therefore the parable of the *sower*.

...he that received seed into the good ground
is he that heareth the word, and understandeth it;
which also beareth fruit, and bringeth forth,
some an hundredfold, some sixty, some thirty.
...The Kingdom of Heaven is likened unto a man
which sowed good seed in his field:
but while men slept, his enemy came
and sowed [weeds] among the wheat,
and went his way...
Let both grow together until the harvest:
and in the time of harvest I will say to the reapers,
gather ye together first the [weeds],
and bind them in bundles *to burn them.*
but gather the wheat into my barn.
Another parable put he forth unto them, saying,
The kingdom of heaven is like a grain of mustard seed,
which a man took, and sowed in his field:
Which indeed is the least of all seeds: but
when it is grown, it is the greatest among herbs,
and becometh a tree, so that the birds of the air come
and lodge in the branches thereof...
He that soweth the good seed is the Son of man;
the field is the world;

the good seed are the children of the kingdom;
but the tares are the children of the wicked one;
the enemy that sowed them is the devil;

the harvest is the *end of the world.*
and the reapers are the angels.
As therefore the tares are gathered
and burned in *the fire;*
so shall it be in the *end of this world.*
The son of man shall send forth his angels,

and they shall gather out of his kingdom
all things that offend,
and them which do iniquity;
and shall cast them into a furnace of fire:
there shall be *wailing and gnashing of teeth.*
Then shall the righteous shine forth as the sun
in the Kingdom of their Father.

Who hath ears to hear let him hear.

So shall it be at the end of this world:
the angels shall come forth, and sever the wicked
from among the just.
And shall cast them into the furnace of fire:
There shall be wailing and gnashing of teeth.
Jesus saith unto them,
have you understood all these things?
They say unto him, Yea, Lord."

Matthew 13:1-5,7-9,12,18,23-25,30-32,37-43,49-51

"Many will say to me in that day, Lord, Lord,
have we not prophesied in thy name?
And in thy name have cast out devils?
And in thy name done many wonderful works?
And then will I profess unto them, I never knew you:
depart from me ye that work iniquity."

Matthew 7:22,23

It appears here that being a 'Sunday-go-to-meeting'
Christian is no guarantee of your soul's salvation, you bet'cha,
unless you die first, in corruption. This is the case for most

people, but what of the remnant of humanity during the time when God manifest again, fulfilling her plan?

If you are religious, then this scripture is extremely important because it makes explicitly clear that it is possible to prophesy and cast out devil's, and do good works, all in God's name; yet, this same God claims, "I never knew you."

This means that just like the Nazis did, and for example, many ministers of the South who attended and attend KKK rallies at night, you can call yourself a Christian, yet Jesus claims that he never knew you. This explains Jesus' dramatic exclamation saying, "depart from me ye that work iniquity." Iniquity is inequality.

"This people draweth nigh unto me with their mouth,
and honoureth me with their lips;
but their heart is far from me.
But in vain do they worship me,
teaching for doctrines the commandments of men."
Matthew 15:8,9

You know, no smoking, no dancing, vote republican, etc.

"Therefore whosoever heareth these *sayings* of mine,
and doeth them, I will liken him unto a wise man,
which built his house upon a rock;
and the rain descended,
and the floods came,
and the winds blew, and beat upon that house;
and it fell not:
for it was founded upon a rock."
Matthew 7:24-25

"**I AM** the light of the world:
he that followeth me shall not walk in darkness,
but shall have the light of life."
John 8:12

"He that rejecteth me, and receiveth not my words,
hath one that judgeth him:
the word that I have spoken,
the same shall judge him *in the last day.*
For I have not spoken of myself;
but the Father which sent me,
he gave me a commandment:
what I should *say, and* what I should *speak,*
And I know that his commandment is *life everlasting:*
whatsoever I speak therefore,
even as the Father said unto me, so I speak."
John 12:48-50

"Verily, verily, I say unto you, he that receiveth
whomsoever I send receiveth me;
and he that receiveth me,
receiveth him that sent me."
John 13:20

Jesus is going to send us a messenger one day. Think of him
or her as the ambassador of GOD. The official office is that
of the Elijah of the second coming. To accept Jesus, you must
accept the messenger of **I AM**. Also, we know that the people
of Jewish faith are awaiting the coming of Elijah. This is why
people of Jewish faith leave a plate for Elijah at the dinner table,
during holidays.

"**I AM** the vine, ye are the branches.
He that abideth in me, and I in him,
the same bringeth forth much fruit:
for without me ye can do nothing.
If a man abide not in me,
he is cast forth as a branch,
and is withered;
and men gather them,
and cast them into the fire;
and they are burned.
If ye abide in me,
and my words abide in you,
ye shall ask what ye will,
and it shall be done unto you.
Herein is my Father glorified,
that ye bear much fruit;
so shall ye be my disciples."

John 15:5-8

"**I AM** like a green fir tree.
From me is thy fruit found.
Who is wise, and he shall understand these things?
Prudent, and he shall know them?
For the ways of the Lord are right,
and the just shall walk in them:
but the transgressors shall fall therein."

Hosea 14:8,9

"...**I AM** the bread of life:
he that cometh to me shall never hunger;
and he that believeth on me shall never thirst...
I AM the living bread which came down from heaven:

If any man eat of this bread,
he shall live forever..."
John 6:35,51

"Verily, verily, I say unto you,
he that entereth not by the door into the sheepfold,
but climbeth up some other way,
the same is a thief and a robber.
But he that entereth in by the door is the shepherd
of the sheep...the sheep hear his voice:
and he calleth his own sheep by name,
and leadeth them out...
And when he putteth forth his own sheep,
he goeth before them, and the sheep follow him:
for they know his voice.
...Verily, verily, I say unto you, **I AM**
the door of the sheep.
All that ever came before me are thieves and robbers:
but the sheep did not hear them.
I AM the door: by me if any man enter in,
he shall be saved, and shall go in and out,
and find pasture...**I AM** come that they might have life,
and that they might have it more abundantly...
I AM the good shepherd, and know my sheep,
and am known of mine."
John 10:1-4,7-10,14

"I AM the way, the truth, and the life:
no man cometh unto the **FATHER** but by me."
John 14:6

"I have said, ye are Gods;
and all of you are children of the most high."
Psalm 82:6 & John 10:34

This is an extraordinarily important scripture. Notice that it is recorded twice; once from the original Psalm, and then reiterated by Jesus himself in his teachings. The text says that we are all Gods. This claim is seen as heretical in organized religion today, and it was perceived as such in Jesus' time. Yet these words stand today as scripture.

Indeed we can see that on a practical basis, we have the power to create but always with our imagination. Creation is an act of imagination. The message here is that we are conscious beings; and that 'consciousness' distinguishes us from other creatures and from ordinary inanimate matter. Human consciousness is a very special attribute, it is what makes us God.

"Every good gift and every perfect is from above,
and cometh down from the **FATHER of lights...**
Of his own will begat he us with the *word of truth*,
that we should be a kind of *firstfruits*
of his creatures."
James 1:17,18

"Have respect unto the **covenant:**
for the dark places of the earth are full of
the habitations of cruelty."
Psalm 74:20

"My **covenant** will I not break,
nor alter the thing that is gone out of my lips."
Psalm 89:34

Where is God?

"A glorious high throne from the *beginning*
is the place of our sanctuary."
Jeremiah 17:12

We can see here again, that the primary destination for God lies at the Alpha pole. The Beginning, is the source and the destination for evolved sentient beings. To go back to the beginning means we must be born again.

"Behold, the days come, saith the Lord GOD,
that I will send a famine in the land,
not a famine of bread, nor a thirst for water,
but of hearing the words of the Lord.
And they shall wander from sea to sea,
and from the north even to the east,
**they shall run to and fro to seek
the word of the Lord,**
and shall not find it."
Amos 8:11,12

Is this not the status of our world today? Are we not all seeking for answers to our problems in life? The biggest problems of which we all face include the problems involved in how we attain self-actualization, and how do we avoid the spiral to the end of life?

"O the depths of the riches both of the wisdom and
knowledge of GOD!
How unsearchable are his judgments,
and his ways past finding out!
For who hath known the mind of the Lord?
Or who hath been his counselor?
For of him, and through him, and to him,
are all things:
to whom be glory for ever and ever.
A-men."
Romans 11:33,34,36

"I know that, whatsoever God doeth,
it shall be forever:
nothing can be put to it,
nor anything taken from it,
that men should fear before him."
Ecclesiastes 3:14

"What if God, willing to shew his wrath,
and to make his power known,
endured with much longsuffering
the vessels of wrath fitted to destruction:
And that he might make known the riches of his glory
on the vessels of mercy,
which he had afore prepared unto glory,
For he will finish the work,
and cut it short in righteousness:
**because a short work will the Lord make
upon the earth.**"

Romans 9:22,23,28

What if God waited patiently for the perfect time, meanwhile developing the context of the story of humankind to the time when God has chosen in her own wisdom as the ideal context to manifest his power to a generation of people, who, seeing God's power, acknowledge that it is God. Apparently, there will be a sudden and dramatic turn in human history to a time when all people in the earth know God.

"Then said Jesus again unto them,
I go my way, and *ye shall seek me,*
and *shall die in your sins:*
whither I go ye cannot come.
...ye are from beneath; **I AM** from above:
ye are of this world; **I AM** *not of this world*."
John 8:21,23

"Simon Peter said unto him, Lord, whither goest thou?
Jesus answered him, whither I go,
thou canst not follow me now;
but thou shalt follow me afterwards."
John 13:36

"Let not your heart be troubled: ye believe in GOD,
believe also in me.
In my Father's house are many mansions:
If it were not so I would have told you.
I go to prepare a place for you.
And if I go to prepare a place for you,
I will come again, and receive you unto myself;
that where **I AM,** there ye may be also...

118

I will not leave you comfortless: **I will come to you.**
Yet a little while, and the world seeth me no more...
Ye have heard how I said unto you,
I go away, and *come again unto you*...
Hereafter I will not talk much with you:
for the prince of this world cometh,
and hath nothing in me."
John 14: 1-3,18,19,28,30

Please consider the meaning in these words with due deliberation. They refer to the history of our world after Christ. It has been over 2,000 years since messiah was slain.

"A little while, and ye shall not see me:
and again, a little while, and ye shall see me,
because I go to the Father."
John 16:16

Why Did God Turn His Back On Us?

"...Because your fathers have
forsaken me, saith the Lord,
and have walked after other Gods,
and have served them,
and have worshipped them,
and have forsaken me,
and have not kept my law;
And ye have done worse than your fathers;
For behold, ye walk every one after the
imagination of his *evil heart,*
that they may not hearken unto me:"
Jeremiah 16:11,12

We see here an account from God's perspective explaining humankind's separation from God. We are conscious beings, hence we are of I AM. The 'break,' or the 'fall' lies in that we are born of God (consciousness) but then we learn to create erroneous thoughts, and follow them.

"Behold, the Lord's hand is not shortened,
that it cannot save;
neither his ear heavy, that it cannot hear:

but your iniquities have hid his face from you,
that he will not hear."

Isaiah 59:1,2

"For a small moment have I forsaken thee:
but with great mercies will I gather thee.
In a little wrath I hid my face from thee for a moment;
but with everlasting kindness will I have mercy on thee,
saith the Lord thy redeemer.
For this is as the *waters of Noah* unto me:
For as I have sworn that the waters of Noah should
no more go over the earth; so have I sworn that I would
not be wroth with thee, nor rebuke thee.
For the mountains shall depart,
and the hills be removed;
but my kindness shall not depart from thee,
neither shall the covenant of my peace be removed,
saith the Lord that hath mercy on thee...
And all thy children shall be taught of the lord;
and great shall be the peace of thy children.
In righteousness shalt thou be established:
thou shalt be far from oppression;
for thou shalt not fear:
and from terror, for it shall not come near thee...
No weapon that is formed against thee shall prosper;
and every tongue that shall rise
against thee in judgment
thou shalt condemn.
This is the heritage of the servants of the Lord,
and their righteousness is of me, saith the Lord."

Isaiah 54:7-10,13,14,17

This is a remarkable vision of a reality in which there is no more oppression, no terror or even the fear of terror.

"Obey my voice, and I will be your God,
and ye shall be my people:
and walk ye in all the ways that I have commanded you,
that it may be well with you.
But they hearkened not, nor inclined their ear,
but walked in the counsels and in the *imagination*
of their evil heart, and went backward,
and not forward.
Since the day that your fathers
came forth out of the land
of Egypt unto this day
I have sent unto you all my servants and prophets,
daily rising up early and sending them:
Yet they hearkened not unto me,
nor inclined their ear,
but hardened their neck:
they did worse than their fathers.
...This is a nation that obeyeth not
the voice of the lord their God,
nor receiveth correction: truth is perished,
and is cut off from their mouth."
Jeremiah 7:23-26,28,2

How Did God Create The Earth

"In the beginning God created the heaven and the earth.
And the earth was without form and void;"

"The earth was without form and void," simply means that in the beginning there was no Earth. This is the story of how the Earth came into being so there was no Earth before it came into being. The story is told from God's perspective—from infinity. So, there is an implicit understanding that the Earth existed perhaps in the mind of the universe, or the mind of God as a possibility, an idea, before it came into being.

It is very important to note that this account of the origin of the Earth states directly that the universe itself, had a beginning because, "in the beginning God created the heaven and the earth."

"And the earth was without form and void;
and darkness was upon the face of the deep."

In the beginning, there was no Earth and it was dark down in the basement of the universe. This is the account of the Earth's origin so the universe is assumed to exist providing the context for a planet body. Remember that the universe is so very big that relativistic principles are at play. Meaning that space can shrink or expand, time can slow or speed up, and there are dimensions of spacetime so far from the here and now that there can be no causal interactions between the here and now and the elsewhere.[18] Of course, this limitation does not necessarily speak to causal relations between the elsewhere and the here and now.

> "And the spirit of God moved upon
> the face of the waters."

The spirit of God, or the consciousness of God, moved thru space and time, examining his basement. I think he has a work project in mind. Remember that this is a time before the Earth even came into being. Consciousness, or the 'observer,' is imagining.

> "And God said, let there be light:
> and there was light."

God turned on the light in a room in the basement of the universe; but had already entered the basement in the dark.

> "And God saw the light, that it was good;
> and God divided the light from the darkness.
> And God called the light Day, and the darkness
> he called Night."

When we transition from the dark spacetime of the hallway in the basement, to the workroom of lighted spacetime, as he walked through the door,

> "And the evening and the morning were the first day."

---

[18] Wolfson, R., *Einstein's Relativity and the Quantum Revolution,* 2nd Ed., p147

The beauty here lies is in the simplicity. God created "day," in the first day.

"And God said, let there be a firmament in the midst of the waters and let it divide the waters from the waters."

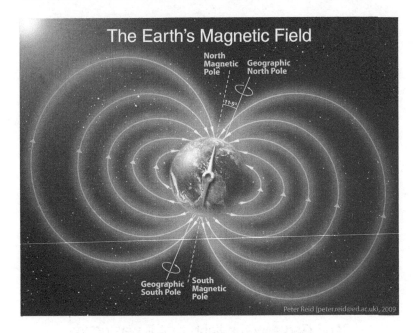

"And God made the firmament,
and divided the waters
which were under the firmament
from the waters which were above
the firmament: *and it was so...*

This artistic rendering[19] demonstrates the Earth's magnetic field as a dramatic dynamic field in which the interplay of the gravitational field lines, *forms the Earth,* like the seed of a fruit. The lines above and below detail the nature and relationship of

---

[19] Peter Reid (peter.reid@ed.ac.uk), 2009

the mirror image poles we call North and South. The Earth's body is formed in a dramatic intertwining of both poles lines of gravity.

The word, 'firmament', in my opinion, refers to the spacetime that forms the Earth's magnetic field. The field is a firmer, more tangible presence than ordinary spacetime, due to the fact that it is bent into the shape of a torus that separates and distinguishes it as an object from the surrounding spacetime milieu.

The 'planet body's gravity field lines run between the North and South poles in a circuit. The lines emanate from the South pole, outward, encircle, then point downward at the North pole. This accounts for due North, and thus the directions up and down, dividing the waters.

The Earth is formed where the lines meet in the center of the torus-shaped system. The circuit is a system that works as an engine to move spacetime to form a concentrate. When time is infused into a specific special location, then that space attains a temporal presence meaning that it becomes more tangible. Overall, relative to the system, there is spacetime above it, below it, and around it.

On the second day: God envisioned a specific set of mirror image poles—probabilities that can spontaneously manifest in the presence of the observer. All that is required is consciousness.

"Consciousness" focuses attention to a specific region of spacetime creating the here and now. Spacetime is infused with quantum fluctuations which are everywhere. Probabilities from the quantum scrim are always present everywhere. North and South mirror image poles are probabilities that can spontaneously pop out of the quantum scrim.

These specific types of poles in communion, creates a circuit that has the power to move the affected spacetime collectively to the region in the middle between the poles. This forms an expanse of interconnected spacetime that is bent introducing gravity and acceleration towards the center.

"And God said, let the waters under the heaven
be *gathered together to one place,"*
and let the dry land appear: *and it was so."*

At the common meeting place in the center, the spacetime, under the immense pull of gravity, coalesces and congeals increasing gravitational pressure, phasing to form the atmosphere, and below that, liquid water; then below that, reality becomes granular. The result of this, the earliest stages of creation, is the simple vision of waters and the sky above; and the sky reflecting off the waters.

The dry land exist because God commanded the spacetime "to be gathered unto one place." Looking down from above, the spacetime first congealed, *way down in the depths*, more and more towards the finite, to "one place," the concentration of time in one place causes spacetime to congeal, to form water. The land became manifested way down in the depths; *below the water*, originating at the most finite scales of infinity. Reality at this level becomes granular, pixilated, sand, dirt.

The lowest dimensions of space and time exist on and at the most finite scales. It is interesting to note that sand, when hit by lightening, becomes glass; which is a very slow liquid and clear, revealing its spatio-temporal origin.

Words are very important because they are tied to our perceptions of reality. Sand, interestingly enough, using it as just another word, exist the first transition from sea to land.

Hence, sand. And to call Earth, 'land,' implies a perspective above in space. The multiple layers of earth's dirt, reflects 'the continuum' nature of the universe; manifesting 'continuum' even at the lowest dimensions of space and time, so we see layers of dirt.

God divided spacetime when he created the Earth's magnetic field. The spacetime of the Earth's magnetic field, turned in onto itself, creating up and down. "Down" is a dimension with it's own peculiar characteristics, and not just a direction. Down is not the same as the directions N, E, W, or S.

The dimension "down" can be understood in this very practical example: on earth one can travel in any direction: N, E, W, or S; but the easiest way to travel down is to *bury internally*. The dimension "down" moves linearly in that direction; simultaneously there are arrows from all directions pointing inward, or internally. The dimension "down" moves downward and inward toward inner space: this is essentially gravity. "Up" moves upward and simultaneously outward, like a cone, toward outer space. This is essentially dark energy.

"Down" means that as you progress in time, there is less and less space and time. Space and time becomes increasingly finite from the scales of infinity; from outer space to inner space. This is the spiraling of the spacetime fabric folding to form the abyss, which is the pit. The funnel from infinity toward inner space is the galactic swirl. The law in this domain is gravity; which for conscious living beings, is the law of the flesh or the body, which leads to death in the end. But, what of the law of the mind?

The pit has a threshold in the same way that the ending has an end. The threshold is what our scientists call, the *event horizon*. When we die and go 6 feet under, the body has died, but though consciousness has no spatial location, it is inextricably linked to time, so it continues traveling down the arrow of time to the end.

The supermassive black hole at the center of the Milky Way, is the end of the circuit. It is approximately 25,000 light years away. This suggest that there is a lot of time left in this very tiny space, relativistically speaking, before the souls that have died cross the event horizon. It is likely here, in the time after death and before one's consciousness reaches the event horizon, that individual consciousnesses that have died are delivered from death, if they are to be delivered. It is likely that this is the domain that is referred to as purgatory.

Warning Will Robinson! The soul dies when there is polarity, which is to say that the end has come to the system because the mirror image poles changed from body and mind, to body or mind. Polarity leads to death of the system. The first death is when we go 6 feet under. The second death occurs when the conscious mind, separated from the body, which is now a corpse, continues to travel the arrow of time to the event horizon of the super-massive black hole at the center of every galaxy. This is the end!

It appears that the lost souls whom are destined for judgment, will be ensconced in spacetime of excruciating gravity, near the mouth of the black hole. The gravity here is as though you had the full weight of the universe on your head forcing you toward the end; but, consciousness never dies. This area is a cauldron of energy, we see quasars emitting huge amounts of the energy because it is a bottleneck situation. The spacetime near the event horizon is hell. Here the conscious experience is excruciating, you are trapped, and it last forever because there is no place to go, ahead, there is no more time.

"And God called the dry land Earth;
and the gathering together of the
waters called he Seas:"
and God saw that it was good.
And God said, let the earth bring forth grass,
the herb yielding seed, and the fruit tree yielding fruit
after its kind, *whose seed is in itself*...
And the evening and the morning were the third day."

In the 4th day: God created the sun in the firmament to rule the day. The stars, and moon, and celestial lights, to rule the night. Remember that relativistic principles are at play when dealing with vast amounts of spacetime. We know that it takes a while for the light to get here now, from the sun. So God created it before, and now it shows up in the present.

On the 5th day: God manifested life forms in the sea and in the air; the fowls of heaven and the fishes of the sea.

On the 6th day: God made the beast of the earth and created man in his own image. Male and female created he them.

On the 7th day: God rested from all his labor, and blessed the Sabbath day. God sanctified the seventh day of the week, making it holy.

"These are the generations of the heavens
and of the earth when they were created,
in the day that the Lord God made the earth
and the heavens"
Genesis 1&2

God felt really good about his work, after making the Earth. He was like, "I really really like that, it's cool!" He felt so good about the Earth knowing of all the amazing possibilities to emerge from it that that he blessed the day after he finished it and enjoyed the rest.

The weeks are seven days long. Saturday is the last day of the week. The Sabbath day is Saturday. Sunday is the first day of the week, it is opposite the Sabbath. Check your calendars.

The Sabbath looks like this: on Friday nights the people settle in at home, no more hustle and bustle. On this day you must do no work for pay, and though there are times when labor may be necessary—unforeseen events, daily activities, etc.; still that day should be set up to minimize need for labor.

The day is meant to be a day of mindfulness. So on this day we focus on the mind, and minimize attention to the body. This behavior over the years will develop a collective superconscious state of mind that has enough space for communion with God. The angels will visit that society. God likes to come to Earth directly on the Sabbaths and engage the society of Earthlings, in all cultures. Remember GOD is the WORD. This means literally that many profound and insightful conversations and ways of learning new things will emerge spontaneously.

They say that there are seven spirits of God in the Earth. So there are seven types of cultures of worship that will evolve over the times ahead that are the seven spirits of God. So what will transpire in the times ahead is that we will become more and more refined beings. Our collective thoughts and sub-conscious processes will change and develop unto higher orders of thoughts in terms of scale. Our thinking will change from linear to holistic. Our minds will become less granular, filling with water. We will become over the next thousand years, a spiritually evolved society.

This is the *first resurrection* and the church that messiah is coming for. I am publishing this thought because of the ignorance of religion-dom. Contrary to the contemporary teachings of todays theologians, it is clearly written in the book of Revelation that Christ is coming in person *after the millennium.*[20]

If Christ were to come before the millennium, why would he need to come again, presumably for the third time, after the millennium? Did he come, create peace then left for war to come back? Is he the prince of peace and war, or is he the prince of peace? If the blind lead the blind, both will fall into the pit.

---

[20] Revelation, chapter 20

Life & Death

"*Death* and *life* are in the *power of the tongue:*
and they that love it shall eat the fruit thereof."
Proverbs 18:21

The wisdom in this proverb is almost obscured. What can this mean? Certainly, if you have read through this book then these words would point to a meaningful and profound understanding. I hope you appreciate your own obligation to your own mind, to your own life.

"The days of our years are threescore years and ten;
and if by reason of strength they be fourscore years,
yet is there strength labour and sorrow;
for it is soon cut off, and we fly away."
Psalm 90:10

The lifespan of humans is 70 – 80 years but much of it is hard work and disappointments, then we die. It is interesting to consider that today, with all our advances in medicine and technology, the human lifespan is consistent with the lifespan that the psalmist wrote of some three millennia ago.

When I was in 8th grade, I took a music class that for some reason stays with me to this day. The teacher, Ms. Crabapple, had us memorize the words to the Beatles' song, *Eleanor Rigby.*

The lyrics go, "Eleanor Rigby died in the church and was buried along with her name. Nobody came. Father McKenzie, wiping the dirt from his hands as he walks from the grave, no one was saved, all the lonely people, where do they all come from, all the lonely people, where do they all belong..."

"My son, forget not my law;
but let thine heart keep my commandments.
For length of days, and long life, and peace,
shall they add to thee."
Proverbs 3:1-2

"In the way of righteousness is life;
and in the pathway thereof,
there is no death."
Proverbs 12:28

"Give instruction to a wise man, and he will be yet wiser;
teach a just man, and he will increase in learning.
The fear of the Lord is the beginning of wisdom:
and the *knowledge of the holy* is understanding.
For by me thy days shall be multiplied,
and the years of thy life shall be increased."
Proverbs 9:9-11

The purpose of this book is to come back to the remembrance of GOD. If you have managed to read this book before reading, *Our Curious World of Mirror Images*, then be aware that the deepest and most profound understandings of the meaning in the phrase Alpha and Omega, are well developed using our most robust knowledge of reality (science), and the intuitive acceptance of our ideas of GOD. Reading this book will really help you to see the world in a new light and understand reality.

"The fear of the Lord is a fountain of life,
to depart from the snares of death...
The way of life is *above* to the wise,
that he may depart from the hell *beneath*...
A fools mouth is his destruction,
and his lips are the snares of his soul."
Proverbs 14:27, 15:24, 18:7

"Because he hath set his love upon me,
therefore will I deliver him.
I will set him on high,
because he hath *known my name*.
He shall call upon me, and I will answer him.
I will be with him in trouble;
I will deliver him and honour him.
With long life will I satisfy him,
and shew him my salvation."
Psalm 91:14-16

"There is therefore now no condemnation
to them which are in Christ Jesus,
who *walketh not after the flesh,*
but after the Spirit."
Romans 8:1

"For they that are after the flesh
do mind the things of the flesh;
but they that are after the Spirit
the things of the Spirit.

For to be carnally minded is death;
but to be spiritually minded is
life and peace."
Romans 8:5,6

"For if we live after the flesh,
ye shall die:
but if ye *through the Spirit*
do mortify the deeds of the body,
ye shall live.
Romans 8:13

"[we are all waiting]...for the manifestation
of the sons of GOD...
Because the creature itself also shall be delivered
from the bondage of corruption into
the glorious liberty of the children of GOD.
For we know that the whole creation
groaneth and travaileth in pain together
until now.
And not only they, but ourselves also,
which are the firstfruits of the Spirit, even we
ourselves groan within ourselves,
waiting for the... redemption of our body.
Likewise the Spirit also helpeth our infirmities:
for we know not what we should pray for
as we ought: but the Spirit itself maketh intercession
for us...for the saints according to the will of GOD.
For whom he did foreknow, he also did
predestinate to be conformed to the image of his Son,
that he might be the firstborn among many brethren.
Romans 8:19, 21-23, 26-27, 29

The Regeneration

"And Jesus said unto them, Verily I say unto you,
that ye which have followed me,
in the *regeneration*
when the Son of man shall sit in the throne of his glory,
ye also shall sit upon twelve thrones, judging
the twelve tribes of Israel.
And every one that hath forsaken houses, or brethren,
or sisters, or father, or mother, or wife,
or children, or lands,
for my names sake,
shall receive an hundredfold,
and *shall inherit everlasting life.*
But many that are first shall be last;
and the last shall be first."
Matthews 19:28-30

I think that it is interesting to note that the one's whom Jesus is speaking to here, are the one's who follow him *in the regeneration.* We see that in this word, 'regeneration,' there is implicit meaning signifying a new beginning. So again we see the Alpha pole, the fountain of the waters of life.

In addition, it is critical to point to the specific times that Jesus is talking about, relative to the way reality had played out in history before. Jesus is speaking about the ones who turn to him *during the times of the regeneration*. But what of the ones who call themselves Christians in the times before this scripture is fulfilled?

"Not by works of righteousness which we have done,
but according to his mercy he saved us,
by the *washing of regeneration*,
and renewing of the Holy Ghost;"

Titus 3:5

"And immediately I was in the spirit:
and, behold, a throne was set in heaven,
and **one** sat on the throne.
And round about the throne were four and twenty seats:
and upon the seats I saw four and twenty elders sitting,
clothed in white raiment;
and they had on their heads crowns of gold.
And out of the throne proceeded
lightenings and thunderings and *voices*:
And there were seven lamps of fire
burning before the throne,
which are the seven spirits of God.
And before the throne there was
a sea of glass like unto crystal;

The four and twenty elders fall down before him
that sat on the throne, and worship him that liveth
for ever and ever,
and cast their crowns before the throne, saying,
Thou art worthy, O Lord, to receive glory
and honour and power:
for thou hast created all things,

and for thy pleasure they are and were created."
Revelation 4:2,4-6,10,11

"Behold, the days come, saith the Lord,
that I will raise undo David a righteous Branch,
and a King shall reign and prosper,
and shall execute judgment and justice in the earth.
In his days, Judah shall be saved
and Israel shall dwell safely:
and this is his name whereby he shall be called,
THE LORD OF OUR RIGHTEOUSNESS.
Therefore, behold, the days come,
saith the Lord, that they shall no more say,
the Lord liveth, which brought up the children
of Israel out of the land of Egypt;
But, the Lord liveth, which brought up and
which led the seed of the house of Israel
out of the north country, and from all
countries whither I had driven them;
and they shall dwell in their own land.
Jeremiah 23:5-8

We are able to determine a sense of the timeframe in which these scriptures refer to, based on the given context. In the text above we see that the Earth will have a righteous king after Israel had been dissolved and reestablished as a nation. In the texts below, we see that the fulfillment of prophecy for the second time occurs in the last days of the present era and that the righteous Earthly king will have the power to change reality with his words; and the Earth will have a renewed spiritual energy and innocence to the extent that no one will kill any living creature.

"And it shall come to pass *in the last days,*
that the mountain of the Lord's house shall be
established in the top of the mountains,
and shall be exalted above the hills;
and *all nations shall flow unto it.*
And many people shall go and say, come ye,
and let us go up to the mountain of the Lord,
to the house of the God of Jacob;
and he will teach us of his ways,
and we will walk in his paths:
for out of Zion shall go forth the law,
and the words of the Lord from Jerusalem.
**And he shall judge among the nations,
and shall rebuke many people:
and they shall beat their swords into plowshares
and their spears into pruninghooks:
nation shall not lift up sword against nation,**
neither shall they learn war anymore."
Isaiah 2:2-4. & Micah 4

"In those days, and at that time,
will I cause the **Branch** of righteousness
to grow up unto David;
**and he shall execute judgment and
righteousness in the land."**
Jeremiah 33:15

"...behold I will bring forth my servant the **Branch.**
For behold the stone that I have laid before Joshua;
upon one stone shall be seven eyes:
Behold, I will *engrave* the graving thereof,
saith the Lord of hosts, and

I will remove the iniquity of that land in one day."
Zechariah 3:8,9

"Thus saith the Lord of host;
I AM jealous for Jerusalem and for Zion
with a great jealously.
And **I AM** very sore displeased with the heathen
that *are at ease*: For I was but a little displeased,
and they helped forward the affliction.
Therefore thus saith the Lord;
I AM returned to Jerusalem with mercies:
My house shall be built in it, saith the Lord of hosts,
And a line shall be stretched forth upon Jerusalem.
Cry yet, saying, thus saith the Lord of hosts;
My cities through prosperity shall yet be spread abroad;
And the Lord shall yet comfort Zion,
And shall yet choose Jerusalem."
Zechariah 1:14-17

"All the people of the land shall give this oblation for
the *prince in Israel.*
And it shall be the prince's part to give burnt offerings...
In the new moons, and in the sabbaths,
in all solemnities of the house of Israel...
Thus saith the Lord God;
the gate of the inner court
that looketh toward the east
shall be shut the six working days;
but on the sabbaths it shall be opened,
and in the day of the new moon it shall be opened.
And the prince shall enter by the way of the porch
of that gate without,

and shall stand by the post of the gate,
and the priests shall prepare his burnt offering
and his peace offerings,
and he shall worship at the threshold of the gate...
Moreover the prince shall not take of the people's
inheritance by oppression,
to thrust them out of their possessions;
but he shall give his sons inheritance
out of his own possessions:
that my people be not scattered
every man from his possessions."
Ezekiel 45:16,17 & 46:1,2,18

And there shall come forth a rod
out of the stem of Jesse,
and a **Branch** shall grow out of his roots:
And the spirit of the Lord shall rest upon him,
and the spirit of wisdom and understanding,
the spirit of counsel and might,
the spirit of knowledge and of the fear of the Lord;
and shall make him of quick understanding in the fear of
the Lord...But with righteousness
shall he **judge the poor,**
and reprove with equity for the meek of the Earth:
and he shall smite the Earth with the rod of his mouth,
and *with the breath of his lips*
shall he slay the wicked...
The wolf also shall dwell with the lamb,
and the leopard shall lie down with the kid;
and a calf and the young lion and the fatling together;
and *a little child shall lead them.*
They shall not hurt nor destroy in all my holy mountain;

for *the earth shall be full of the knowledge*
of the Lord, as the waters cover the sea.
And it shall come to pass in that day,
that the Lord shall set his hand again
the **second** time to recover the remnant of his people..."
Isaiah 11:1-4,6,9,11

"And I will strengthen the house of Judah,
and I will save the house of Joseph,
and I will bring them *again* to place them;
for I have mercy upon them;
and they shall be as though I
had not cast them off:
for **I AM** the Lord their **GOD,** and will hear them.
I will hiss for them, and gather them;
for I have redeemed them...

...and they shall *remember me* in far countries;
and they shall live with their children, and *turn again.*
And I will strengthen them in the Lord;
and they shall walk up and down **in his name,**
saith the Lord."
Zechariah 10:6,8,9,12

"For the Lord shall comfort Zion:
he will comfort all her waste places;
and he will make all her wilderness like Eden,
and all her desert like the garden of the Lord;
joy and gladness shall be found therein,
thanksgiving, and the voice of melody.
Hearken unto me, my people; and give ear unto me,
O my nation: for a law shall proceed from me,

and I will make my judgment to rest
for a light of the people.
My righteousness is near; my salvation is gone forth,
and mine arms shall judge the people;
the isles shall wait upon me,
and on mine arm shall they trust.
Therefore the redeemed of the Lord shall return,
and come with singing unto Zion; and
everlasting joy shall be upon their head:
they shall obtain gladness and joy...
I, even **I AM** he that **comforteth** you:"
Isaiah 51:3-5,11,12

"Ho, every one that thirsteth, *come ye to the waters,*
and he that hath no money;
come ye, buy, and eat; yea, come,
buy wine and milk without money
and without price.
Incline your ear, and come unto me:
Hear, and your soul shall live;
and I will make an everlasting covenant with you,
even the sure mercies of David.
Seek ye the Lord while he may be found,
Call ye upon him while he is near:
Let the wicked forsake his way,
and the unrighteous man his **thoughts:**
and let him return unto the Lord;
and he will have mercy upon him; and to our GOD,
for he will abundantly pardon.
For *my thoughts are not your thoughts,*
neither are your ways my ways, saith the Lord.
For as the heavens are higher than the earth,

so are my ways higher than your ways,
and my thoughts than your thoughts.
For as the rain cometh down, and
the snow from heaven,
and...watereth the earth, and maketh
it bring forth and **bud,**
that it may give **seed to the sower,**
and bread to the eater:
**So shall my word be that goeth
forth out of my mouth;"**
Isaiah 55:1,3,6-11

"Behold, I will take the children of Israel from among
the heathen, whither they be gone,
and will gather them on every side,
and bring them into their own land:
and I will make them one nation in the land
upon the mountains of Israel;
and one king shall be king to them all:
and they shall be no more two nations,
neither shall they be divided into two kingdoms
any more at all. Neither shall they defile themselves
any more with their idols,
nor with their detestable things,
nor with any of their transgressions:
but I will save them out of all their dwelling-places,
wherein they have sinned,
and will cleanse them: so shall they be my
people, and I will be their GOD.
And David my servant shall be king over them;
and they all shall have one shepherd:
they all shall walk in my judgments,

and observe my statutes, and do them...
Moreover I will make a covenant of peace with them;
It shall be an everlasting covenant with them:
And I will place them, and multiply them, and
will set my sanctuary in the midst of them for evermore.
My tabernacle also shall be with them:
Yea, I will be their GOD, and they shall be my people.
And the heathen shall know that I the Lord do
sanctify Israel, when my sanctuary shall be
in the midst of them for evermore.

Ezekiel 37: 21-24, 26-28

The Trinity

The word, 'universe,' means "one united verse," or, "one sentence." Can you tell me of everything in one sentence, one phrase? What is the fundamental thing that accounts for all of reality? That thing as I have identified it in this book is, 'ALPHA & OMEGA.' All things visible and invisible exists within the context of this word, whose meaning forms space and time, whose name implies consciousness and means, 'Being.' That name of course is, 'I AM'.

GOD is the beginning and the end. Alpha and Omega are words whose meaning refers to an entity that is omnipresent, invisible, and entirely conscious. Spacetime forms its body, which is getting bigger because the Alpha pole is inflating the universe. The galaxies are the Omega pole. Time moves from the beginning to the end, this is a comprehensive account for the arrow of time. The torus-shaped circuit is unbroken so spacetime fills the void. The end has an ending; this is the gravity of dark matter.

The seas are as material representations of the cosmic ocean. All the various types of creatures manifested in the seas, may see and experience some "thing" or another, but many may never really appreciate or even acknowledge, the *water*. As a consequence of this implicit ignorance, God manifest also as a person; so that all other creatures may have a direct person, representing God, to interact with. This of course is the Lord Yeshua the messiah. Yeshua is God's presence and intelligence, manifested in a physical living creature; he is the person of God.

> "Who is the image of the invisible God,
> the first born of *every* creature:
> for by him were all things created,
> that are in heaven, and that are in the earth,
> visible and invisible,
> whether they be thrones, or dominions,
> or principalities, or powers;
> all things were created by him, and for him:
> And he is before all things,
> and by him all things consist.
> And he is the head of the body, the church:
> who is the *beginning,* the firstborn from the dead;
> that in all things he might have the preeminence."
> ### Colossians 1:15-18

We see here that Yeshua, "who is the beginning," is the person representing the Alpha pole of the Alpha and Omega. The **Holy Spirit** is the presence of Alpha's divine spirit in the earth. It is dark energy from the beginning.

I wonder what happens when dark energy is infused into a constricted space? Should the Alpha pole breathe its breath unto the restrictive spaces of the Earth, then history would change and new events would play out leading to the emergence of the **"John the Baptist,"** or **Elijah**; of the **second coming**. This is the fulfillment of numerous biblical prophecies: Psalm 94:12-15, 132:17-18; Obadiah 1:21; Micah 4:1-3/Isaiah 2:2-4; Isaiah 32, 40:1-5, 52:7-15; Jeremiah 23:1-6, 29:8-15, 33:6-9 & 12-16. Please, read them all.

"Why then say the scribes that Elias must first come?.
And Jesus answered and said unto them,
Elias truly shall first come,
and *restore* all things."
Matthew 17:10,11

John the Baptist fulfilled the role of Elijah for the first coming. He ended up with his head chopped off. This makes it very clear that the prophecies of Elijah have not been fulfilled, in full; and it is without question that the church is in need of restoration. We all know that all of the institutions of organized religion are grotesquely corrupt.

"A good tree cannot bring forth evil fruit,
neither can a *corrupt* tree bring forth good fruit.
Every tree that bringeth not forth
good fruit is hewn down
and *cast into the fire*."
Matthew 7:18,19

Elijah is coming to restore the church and his presence means that the judgment that initiates the millennium reign of the Lord, Yeshua ha moshiach, is near. In these times, when God's consciousness is present again in the Earth, as in biblical times, this is the Holy Spirit of prophecy.

"For this is he, of whom it is written, Behold, I send
my messenger before thy face,
which shall prepare the way before thee...
And if you will receive it, this is **Elias,**

which was for to come.
He that hath ears to hear, let him hear."
Matthew 11:10,14-15

"Behold, I will send **my messenger,**
and he shall prepare the way before me:
...even the messenger of the
covenant, whom ye delight in:
behold, he shall come, saith the **Lord of hosts.**
And he shall sit as a refiner and purifier...
..And I will come near to you to judgment;"
Malachi 3:1,3,5

"Howl ye; for the **day of the Lord** is at hand;
it shall come as a **destruction** from the **Almighty.**
Behold, the **day of the Lord** cometh,
cruel both with wrath and fierce anger,
to lay the land desolate:
And **he shall destroy the sinners thereof out of it."**
Isaiah 13:6,9

"For, behold, the day cometh,
that shall burn as an oven;
and all the proud, yea, and all that do wickedly,
shall be stubble: and
the day that cometh shall burn them up,
saith the Lord of hosts,
that it shall leave them neither **root** nor *branch*...
Behold, I will send you **Elijah** the prophet before
the coming of the great and dreadful **day of the Lord:**
and he shall turn the heart of the fathers to the children,
and the heart of the children to their fathers,

lest I come and smite the Earth with a curse."
Malachi 4:1,5

Today the churches of organized religion are anticipating the return of messiah to rapture these people who call themselves Christians, away. If messiah were to come now, who then would he be coming for; for you see he is coming for a perfect church.

"a glorious church, not having spot or wrinkle,
or any such thing;
but that it should be holy and without blemish."
Ephesians 5:27

Any honest person understands that the church today is morally bankrupt. There is no need to mention specifics, sufficient to say that we are all aware of the corrupt condition of organized religion; even the one's who maintain denial. The human beings who compose the church of God, which is the only church, are the ones who have been refined over the 1000 years and are acceptable to God. They survived the first judgment; there is a second and final judgment after the millennium.

The *millennial elect* will experience the *first resurrection;* they develop a society of individuals who are purified and refined as they grow and develop their minds unto higher sentient order and attain true righteousness, which is of God. In my understanding today, I think that the standard for the righteousness that is of God, is probably about 200 years of growth and development in the spirit.

"And they shall be mine, saith the Lord of hosts,
in that day when I make up my jewels;

and *I will spare them,*
as a man spareth his own son that serveth him.
Then shall ye...
discern between the righteous and the wicked,
between him that serveth GOD
and him that serveth him not."
Malachi 3:17,18

It is in these times in Earth's history, when we will be able to really see the difference between God's people, and the people who are too rebellious to submit to God. Today, there is good and evil in all of us, none of us are clean. Then, there will be clean people and we will see the differences between the good people and the evil people.

"And I saw an angel come down from heaven,
having the key of the bottomless pit and a
great chain in his hand.
And he laid hold of the dragon,
that old *serpent,*
which is the Devil, and Satan,
and bound him a thousand years,
And cast him into the bottomless pit,
and shut him up,
till the thousand years should be fulfilled:
and after that he must be loosed a little season...
And when the thousand years are expired,
Satan shall be loosed out of his prison,
and shall go out to
deceive the nations...to gather them together to battle:
And they went up on the breadth of the earth, and
compassed the camp of the saints about,

and the beloved city;
and *fire came down from God out of heaven,
and devoured them.*
And the devil that deceived them was
cast into the lake of fire and brimstone,
where *the beast* and the **false prophet** are,
and shall be tormented day and night for ever and ever."
Revelation 20: 1-3, 7-10

The **beast** is an archetype representing the governments of humanity and their armies (state); which, due to their propensity for war and cruelty, are as ravenous beast in the eyes of a loving God.

"Who is like unto the beast?
Who is able to make **war** with him?"
Revelation 13:4

The **false prophet** is an archetype representing all false religions including the one's who call themselves Christians. Jesus made it very clear that it is not about him, but about I AM. Jesus informed us that we will know of his disciples "by their love," not by their religion; and also by their behavior because they will do the bidding of I AM.

Note that the scriptures confirm that the beast and the false prophet are already judged, that is because they were judged at the beginning of the millennial reign when the power of the End is subsumed by the new Beginning. So, the vision above includes a time gap of one millennium of love and peace, good foods, great company, wine, biscuits, love, did I mention peace?

Judgment, like all things in reality and in the bible, is a two-fold event. There is judgment at the beginning, and at the end of the millennium reign. The meaning behind this lies in that these are evolutionary stages in our development unto spiritual beings. So there will come an end, coupled with a new beginning.

In the pre-millennial judgment, the **beast** (cruel governments), the **false prophet** (televangelists and other religious leaders), and the culture of **Babylon** (tall buildings – tower of babel, statues everywhere – idol worship, and consumerism), come to an end.

The two institutions of *Church* and *State* will be held accountable by God for the condition of humanity because they are trans-generational sentient entities (a way of being within the collective consciousness of society) that represent power and authority. These two institutions have dealt treacherously against God in the past; and will attempt again in the future. **Messiah** will judge them at the beginning of his reign as **King** of the universe.

The post-millennial judgment appears to be a necessary thing in evolution and the stages of development. We truly are very finite beings, near the dust. To evolve spiritually requires that we must infuse more of the Alpha pole into our consciousness.

The mind, like all existing things, is traveling down the arrow of time toward the end. With each year we live, we are one year closer to the end. The conscious mind must therefore actively access energy from the beginning. This is God, the fountain of living waters.

The millennium reign is very important because this is the time when God finally has his people in the Earth, fulfilling his dominion over all reality. All of the Earth will be in obedience to GOD, so all things will have a consciousness that the universe sustains. The inhabitants will live happily. The Earth will produce an abundance of goods. Humans will live long prosperous lives, and grow in wisdom and understanding.

Very interesting new forms of consciousness and thoughts will emerge creating a universe of words and realities that are all good; and there are good endings.

We will still see an interplay between the beginning of events and the ending, we will still have an active dynamic system of events, but with no negative emotions, only love and wellbeing.

The Earth will be filled with organic cultures of human life accomplishing noble goals. Given this context, then, societies around the world will blossom in peace and harmony. This generation will become refined sentient beings waiting on Jah Jah. *This is the true church.*

One thousand years of harmony and beauty, love and peace, and an abundance of goods, but, to evolve from flesh and blood to spirit requires stages of development. The arrow of time continues from beginning to end. So this is the upward and outward arc of the arrow of time in the times ahead.

All the years of history in this era will occupy more and more spacetime from the beginning and originating off high order. As a consequence, we will enter higher and higher scales requiring stages of development. When the next stage comes, unfortunately, like the reemergence of the id in the adolescent years, we will see Satan again; but, it is short and for the last time.

Near the end of the millennium, after so much peace and love, I can imagine a scenario in which some archeologists find and dig up fragments of a past society. This begins talk about the way it was before the millennium. We went to the moon! Some people become aroused, blah blah, blah, blah blah. When messiah comes back *in person,* he will take his children, destroy this world, judge the dead, and translate us to a new and higher-scale reality; to the extent that our view of the heavens will change.

Our spiritual evolution requires that we literally get away from the influence of the black hole to access higher spacetime and consciousness. We are to be drawn closer to the beginning. We are to seek the dark energy of the Alpha pole. We are to seek the fountain of living waters.

> "And I saw a great white thrown, and him that
> sat on it, from whose face *the earth*
> *and heaven fled away;*
> and there was found no place for them...

This means that Christ, in the glory of **I AM**, is a huge celestial being; on a scale to blot out the heavens, from our earthly point of view.

> And I saw the dead, small and great, stand before God;
> and the *books were opened*: ...
> and the dead were judged out of those things
> written in the books, according to their works."
> **Revelation 20:11-12**

Since God is God over all things, he will judge every soul that lived and died, based on who we are, what we said, and what we did. This is about the intent of the heart, and our behavior given the situations that we inherit and live in.

> "...and his name is called, **THE WORD OF GOD.**
> And the armies which were in heaven followed him
> upon white horses, clothed in fine linen,
> white and clean.

And out of his mouth goeth a sharp sword,
that with it he should smite the nations:
and he shall rule them with a rod of iron:"
Revelation 19:13-15

"And **four** great beast came up from the sea,
diverse one from another.
The first was like a lion, and had eagle's wings...
And behold another beast, a second, like a bear...
After this I beheld, and lo another, like a leopard...
After this I saw in the *night visions*, and behold
a **fourth** beast, dreadful and terrible,
and strong exceedingly;
and it had great iron teeth: it
devoured and brake in pieces,
and stamped the residue with the feet of it:
and it was diverse from all the beast that were before it;
and it had ten horns."
Daniel 7:3-7

The fourth beast represents the armies of the world after the industrial revolution. All of the armies of the world before this time were essentially organic derivatives of horsemen on horseback.

We are all witnesses to the power of these scriptures fulfilled in World War 1, World War 11, and the present state of affairs. This beast is a mechanical army: tanks and armor, warships, rockets, guns, bullets, etc.

"I considered the horns, and, behold, there came up
among them another little horn,
before whom there were

three of the first horns plucked up by the roots:
and, behold, in this horn were eyes like the eyes
of man, and a mouth *speaking great things.*
I beheld till the thrones were cast down,
and the *Ancient of days* did sit,
whose garment was white as snow,
and **the hair of his head like the pure wool:**
his throne was like the fiery flame,
and his wheels as burning fire.
A fiery stream issued and came forth from before him:
thousands ministered unto him, and ten thousand
stood before him: the judgment was set,
and the books opened."

Daniel 7:8-9

"These great beast, which are four,
are four kings, which shall arise out of the earth.
But the saints of the most High shall take the kingdom,
and possess the kingdom for ever,
even for ever and ever.
Then I would know the truth of the fourth beast, which
was diverse from all the others, exceedingly dreadful,
whose teeth were of iron, and his nails of brass;
which devoured, break in pieces,
and stamped the residue with his feet;
And of the ten horns that were in his head,
And of the other which came up, and before whom
three fell; even of that horn that had eyes, and a
mouth that spake very great things, whose look was
more stout than his fellows. I beheld, and the same
horn made war with the saints, and
prevailed against them;

Until the *Ancient of days* came, and judgment
was given to the saints of the most
High; and the time came
that the saints possessed the kingdom.
...the fourth beast shall be the fourth kingdom
upon earth, which shall be diverse from all kingdoms,
and shall devour the whole earth,
and shall tread it down, and break it in pieces."

Daniel 7:17-23

These horns represent great civilizations of the past and present in the Earth as they developed organically. I do not know which specific nations that the ten horns represent but I think I recognize the little horn that was plucked up out of three horns, the one that had great eyes to see things and spoke great things. This horn, or society, think of it as a blip on the cosmic map, is undoubtedly America, or rather, the Americas.

The Americas include, Canada (French), Central America (Spain), and America (England). America is the third horn, composed of three transplanted horns. It is stouter than the others, with sharp consciousness (the eye) and speaking great things. This notion of the horn having eyes and speaking great things refers to science, critical thinking, the enlightenment, etc. Today we can refer to specific technical achievements that fall within the context of these words. Satellites are a product of science and technology, they literally serve us as eyes in the sky. Science, as a method of consciousness, is a lens that has brought forth amazing revelations in terms of our understanding of how reality works.

"And in the days of these kings shall
the GOD of heaven set up a kingdom,

which shall never be destroyed:
and the kingdom shall not be left to other people,
but is shall break in pieces and consume
all these kingdoms, and it shall stand forever."

Daniel 2:44

"Here is wisdom. Let him that hath
understanding count the number of the beast:
for it is the number of a man; and his number
is Six hundred threescore and six.

Revelation 13:18

As for the one for whom, the number of his name is 666; you have to have wisdom to understand it, but the clue is in the number of his name. This is the KKK! The KKK is triple 6.

"And after these things I saw another angel come down
from heaven, having great power;
and the earth was lightened with his glory.
And he cried mightily with a strong voice, saying,
Babylon the great is fallen, is fallen, and is become
the habitation of devils, and the hold of every foul spirit,
and a cage of every unclean and hateful bird...

I think that the meaning here is that the cities of the world have been built by fallen societies. There is good and evil everywhere in the Earth, but with the development of cities, then the cross-pollination of all kinds of thoughts becomes prevalent and evil thoughts are spread throughout the consciousnesses of the constituents.

This means that the cities have become the homes of all well-developed evil thoughts, festering in the hearts of humankind: thoughts of ill-will toward others. You know, we have insight into them when we browse the internet and watch or read the news. The evil thoughts that emerge in this way-of-consciousness, are all alive in our collective subconscious minds, and they have their own agenda according to intent.

All thoughts are alive in us because we are living beings. An evil spirit is a bad thought sown in one's heart that has matured over time to the point that it has its own identity. This thought has matured and has its own personality according to what it is. It aims to fulfill its intent; and has the power to enter into the mind, intrusively, revealing itself. The mind is its home. Humanity, then become the hosts when we obey and serve evil desires fulfilling ill intent toward self or others.

We see this manifested daily. Recently in the news, two young college kids, male and female, thought it a delight to kill a 13 year-old girl for no reason but the pleasure. In another example, a 40 year-old man goes on a shooting spree killing several people and injuring more, for no discernible reason other than it is in his heart to do it.

Come out of her my people,
that ye be not partakers of her sins,
and that ye receive not of her plagues.
For her sins have reached unto heaven,
and God hath remembered her iniquities...
How much she hath glorified herself,
and lived deliciously, so much torment
and sorrow give her...
Therefore shall her plagues come in one day,
death, and mourning, and famine;
and she shall be utterly burned with fire:
for strong is the Lord God who judgeth her.

...Alas, alas, that great city Babylon, that mighty city!
For in one hour is thy judgment come.
And the merchants of the earth shall
weep and mourn over her;
for *no man buyeth their merchandise* any more:
The merchandise of gold, and silver,
and precious stones,
and of pearls, and fine linen, and purple, and silk,
and scarlet, and all thyine wood,
and all manner vessels of ivory,
and all manner vessels of most precious wood,
and of brass, and iron, and marble, and cinnamon,
and odours, and ointments, and frankincense,
and wine, and oil, and fine flour, and wheat,
and beasts, and sheep,
and horses, and chariots,
and slaves, and the souls of men."

Revelation 18:1-13

Wow! I am sure that the folks on Wall Street will not support this biblical passage whether they call themselves Christians or not. Now we know and recognize Babylon. She is no longer a mystery. Babylon is a culture, a way of life defined by consumerism, statues everywhere, and slavery. This is a shapshot of the world that we live in today. Just stand at the grocery store checkout line and look at the magazines that our children have to see every day. The chariots and slaves, and the souls of men, refers to automobiles, slaves, and the souls of men.

The **Holy Spirit** is the spirit of God in the Earth. It is surely a long-term breath from the Alpha pole, emanating through the galaxy into the Earth. This literally means plenty of rain, and floods, etc. The 'meaning' in the waters would stir up new events in the Earth to sustain the presence of the Holy Spirit.

The "John the Baptist" of the second coming would emerge in history; this is the forerunner of messiah, heralding in the millennial reign in the Earth. His presence locks in the *SPIRIT* of God in the earth; as in biblical times when Elijah walked the earth. Now, GOD will have an ambassador in the Earth. This is very important because Jesus alludes to Elijah, who will judge the Earth. But what about the times until this event is realized,

...Hereafter I will not talk much with you:
for the prince *of this world* cometh,
and hath nothing in me."
John 14:30

King Yeshua is no longer a small human imbued with the spirit of God, he is presently in the glory of his father. Ascended up into heaven, he is huge and infinitely powerful; he is **I AM**. Therefore, when he was with us he said,

"And if any man hear my words, and believe me not,
I judge him not: for I came not to judge the world,
but to save the world."
John 12:47

"And I seek not mine own glory:
there is one that seeketh and judgeth."
John 8:50

"And I will pray the Father, and he shall give you
another **Comforter,**
that he may abide with you forever;

Even the Spirit of truth; whom the world cannot receive,"
John 14:16,17

"But the **Comforter,** which is the **Holy Ghost,**
whom the **Father** will send in my name,
he shall teach you all things,
and bring all things to your remembrance,
whatsoever I have said unto you.
John 14:26

"But when the **Comforter** is come,
whom I will send unto you from the **Father,**
even the Spirit of truth,
which proceedeth from the **Father,**
he shall testify of me:"
John 15:26

"But now I go my way to *him that sent me...*
Nevertheless I tell you the truth;
it is expedient for you that I go away: for
if I go not away, the **comforter** will not come unto you;
but if I depart, I will send him unto you.
And when he is come, he will reprove the world of sin,
and of righteousness, and of judgment...
Howbeit when he, the Spirit of truth, is come,
he will guide you into all truth:
...and he shall show you things to come.
He shall glorify me: for he shall receive of mine,
and shall shew it unto you.
...he shall take of mine, and shall show it unto you.
A little while, *and ye shall not see me:*
and again, a little while, and ye shall see me,

because I go to the **Father.**
...I came forth from the **Father,** and
am come into the world;
again, I leave the world, and go to the **Father."**
John 16:5, 7-8,13-16,28

"And I will raise me up a faithful priest,
that shall do according to that which is in mine heart
and in my mind: and I will build him a sure house;
and he shall walk *before mine anointed* forever.
And it shall come to pass, that every one that is left
in thine house shall come and crouch to him
for a piece of silver and a morsel of bread, and shall say,
put me, I pray thee, into one of the priest's offices,
that I may eat a piece of bread."
1 Samuel 2:35,36

"I have raised up *one* from the north,
and *he shall come:*
from the rising of the sun shall he call upon my name...
Who hath declared from the
beginning, that we may know?
And beforetime, that we may say,
He is righteous? Yea, ...
The *first* shall say unto Zion, behold them:
*and I will give to Jerusalem one that bringeth
good tidings."*
Isaiah 41:25-27

"Thus saith the Lord, thy redeemer,
and he that formed thee from the womb,
I AM the Lord that maketh all things;

that *stretcheth forth the heavens alone;*
that spreadeth abroad the earth by myself...
That confirmeth the word of his servant,
and performeth the counsel of his messengers;
...saying to Jerusalem, thou shalt be built;
and to the **temple,**
thy foundation shall be laid."
Isaiah 44:24,26,28

"Behold my servant, whom I uphold; mine elect,
in whom my soul delighteth;
I have put my spirit upon him:
he shall bring forth judgment to the Gentiles.
...he shall bring forth *judgment* unto truth.
He shall not fail nor be discouraged,
till he have set judgment in the earth:
and the isles shall wait for his law."
Isaiah 42:1,3,4

"Behold the man whose name is The **Branch;**
and *he shall grow up out of his place,*
and he shall build the temple of the Lord:
even he shall build the temple of the Lord;
and he shall bear the glory,
and shall sit and rule upon his throne;
and he shall be a priest upon his throne: and
the counsel of peace
shall be between them both.
And they that are far off shall come and build in the
temple of the Lord, and ye shall know
that the Lord of hosts hath sent me unto you.
And this shall come to pass, if ye will diligently obey

166

the voice of the Lord your God."
Zechariah 6:12,13,15

"...what are these **two olive trees** upon the right side
of the candlestick and upon the left side thereof?
...what be these **two olive branches** which through
the two golden pipes empty the
golden oil out of themselves...
These are the *two anointed ones*,
that stand by the Lord of the whole earth."
Zechariah 4:11-14

"Thus saith the Lord my God;
'*feed the flock of the slaughter*';
whose possessors slay them,
and hold themselves *not guilty*:
and *they that sell them* say,
blessed be the Lord; for I am rich:
and their shepherds pity them not...
And I will *feed the flock of the slaughter*,
even you, O *poor* of the flock.
And I took unto me *two staves*;
the **one** I called **Beauty,** and the **other** I called **Bands;**
and I fed the flock."
Zechariah 11: 4,5,7

As with all things concerning the universe, there will be
two representatives. Jesus is beautiful, and Bands has the
power to bind evil thoughts. I think that it is important to pause
here. I will ask you to appreciate the context present in these
words. The 'flock of the slaughter,' refers to a people who were
possessed by others, in other words, they were slaves.

Apparently, their masters were extremely cruel, as evidenced by the fact that they murdered the people under their dominion and thought nothing of it. They apparently bought and sold these people with implicit acceptance by the clergy who thanked God for the wealth.

The Antichrist

The doctrine of the coming of the antichrist, commonly taught today by our religious leaders, is false doctrine. The antichrist(s) have been here since the time of Christ. They were the ones who applied political and social forces to get rid of Jesus, whom they despised.

> "...ye have heard that *antichrist* shall come,
> even now are there *many antichrists;*...
> They went out from us, but they were not of us,...
> they went out, that they might be made manifest
> that they were not all of us.
> Who is a liar but he that denieth that Jesus is the
> Christ? *He is antichrist, that denieth the Father*
> and the Son."
> **1 John 2:18,19,22**

> "Beloved, believe not every spirit, but try the spirits
> whether they are of God: because *many false prophets
> are gone out into the world.*
> ...every spirit that confesseth not that Jesus Christ
> is come in the flesh is not of God:
> and *this is the spirit of* **antichrist,**
> whereof ye have heard that it should come;
> and *even now already is it in the world."*

1 John 4:1,3

"For many deceivers are entered into the world,
who confess not that Jesus Christ is come in the flesh.
This is a deceiver and *an antichrist*."

2 John 1:7

The antichrist exists in the power of the religious leaders of the churches who teach of God during the times of Earth's history that Jesus alluded to, saying, and I paraphrase, "the boss of this world is coming, we have nothing in common."

These false teachers fill the void in the absence of God's immediate presence; and when God manifest again in the Earth fulfilling prophecy, they reject God, and have *killed his messengers* to keep their own gig going.

In the time of **Yeshua**, it was the religious leaders who rejected the message of God, and crucified **Yeshua**. Then, after his death, they talk about Jesus and him crucified. They love this moment, they hold it dear to their religious faith; yet this moment refers to the very worst in Earth's history, when we extinguished the light.

"For they being ignorant of God's righteousness,
and going about to establish their own righteousness,
have not submitted themselves unto the righteousness
that is of God."

Romans 10:3

"Go, and tell this people,
hear ye indeed, but understand not;
and see ye indeed, but perceive not.
Make the heart of this people fat,

and make their ears heavy,
and shut their eyes; lest they see with their eyes,
and hear with their ears, and
understand with their heart,
and convert, and be healed.

Isaiah 6:9,10

The religious leaders sought to bring an end to the presence of Jesus in the Earth, despite the fact the Jesus was peaceful, very wise, and GOD was manifested by the miracles. Despite all this, they not only instigated the activities that brought about Jesus' crucifixion, but they conspired to destroy him even when they had opportunity to save Yeshua's life.

It is important to understand that Jesus was a Jew. To say that the Jews killed Jesus is like saying that America killed JFK. It's true, but not informative. The entire story of Jesus is in the context of Israel's history. If the Jews killed Jesus, and Jesus is a Jew, which one is of greater value? What I am getting at here is acknowledging that the blame for Jesus' death lies at the hands of the religious leaders.

The beast during Roman times, knew that messiah was innocent and offered to free him. But the religious leaders insisted that **Yeshua**, the son of the living God, the messenger of **I AM**, whom they taught to the people every sabbath was coming; the religious leaders insisted that he be condemned.

"When the morning was come,
all the chief priests and elders of the people
took counsel against Jesus to
put him to death:
"And when he was accused of the
chief priests and elders,

he answered nothing...
Now at that feast the governor was
wont to release unto the people a prisoner,
whom they would...
Pilate said unto them, whom will ye
that I release unto you?
Barabbas, or Jesus which is called Christ?
For he knew that for envy they had delivered him.
When he was set down on the judgment seat,
his wife sent unto him, saying,
have nothing to do with that just man:
for I have suffered many things this day in a dream
because of him.
But the *chief priest* and the **elders**
persuaded the multitude that they should ask Barabbas,
and *destroy* Jesus.
When Pilate saw that he could prevail nothing,
but that rather a tumult was made,
he took water,
and washed his hands before the multitude,
saying, I am innocent of the blood of this just person:
see ye to it. Then answered all the people, and said,
His blood be on us, and on our children."
Matthew 27: 1,12,15,17-20,24,25

"Pilate therefore went forth again, and saith unto them,
behold, I bring him forth to you, that ye may know
that I find no fault in him.
...And Pilate saith unto them, behold the man!
When the chief priests therefore and officers saw him,
they cried out saying, *crucify him, crucify him.*
Pilate saith unto them, take ye him and crucify him;

for I find no fault in him...
And from thenceforth Pilate sought to release him...
But they cried out, away with him, away with him,
crucify him.
Pilate saith unto them, shall I crucify your King?
The chief priests answered,
we have no king but Caesar."
John 19:4,6,12,15

The record reveals that the **false prophet** conspired with the **beast** to destroy the messenger of GOD. This is the antichrist in power, they reject the Father and the Son. The people loved Jesus because he was wise, had good parties, and there were spontaneous miracles; but the religious authorities rejected him out of fear that they would lose their own status as the religious elite in society. As a consequence, they rejected Jesus and therefore rejected GOD.

The antichrist is not a singular person to come, as is commonly taught in the churches; though it may involve a figurehead in the course of history; it is ironically, the power of religiondom to maintain their own status in society by destroying God's messengers, when they should appear. This is very important because they will *attempt* to do the very same thing when next we see God. Also, this is why they are telling you that the antichrist is coming. Shouldn't they be teaching us that GOD is coming.

This coming, the second coming, is in the spirit of judgment, not just the mercy and truth of the first coming. Also, Jesus was perfect yet the religious leaders crucified him. This pays the price for redemption because, now, the ascendant Christ bridges the divide between infinity and mortal beings. It is in this transcendent role that messiah guarantees reality for his people in the here and now, and as a consequence, the antichrist will be denied the power to act against God victoriously. The antichrists have great power but that power will be broken by, GOD. Ultimately, this is about the Beginning saying to the End, "chill out, I got this aiight!"

In the first coming, they slew **Elijah,** severing **John the Baptist's** head; and crucified **Yeshua.** This is why Yeshua spoke of judgment against those who even speak out against the **Holy Spirit** (in his time), saying that they are in danger of hellfire. Also clearly, because **Elijah** was slain in the first coming, the prophecies concerning **Elijah** have yet to be fulfilled in full.

"And other sheep I have, which are not of this fold:
them also I must bring, *and they shall hear my voice*;
and there shall be one fold, and one shepherd."

John 10:16

It is stated clearly in scripture that even then, some 2000 years ago, that there are antichrists present. The antichrist is therefore not a figure to come; but an historical figure, whose origins go back to the denial of **Yeshua**, and the rejection of GOD.

"And upon a set day Herod, arrayed in royal apparel,
sat upon his throne, and made an oration unto them.
And the people gave a shout, saying,
It is the voice of a God, and not of man.
And immediately the angel of the Lord smote him,
because he gave not God the glory:
and he was eaten of worms,
and gave up the ghost."

Acts 12:21-23

If the church insist on there being a person to the antichrist, then they must acknowledge that "the antichrist" is endemic to **institutional** religiondom. Also, if, as they say, the antichrist is coming to build his world religion, will it be bigger than the dominant world religions of the 21ˢᵗ century? And won't the present religious powers have something to say about his presence? And who are they to know, given the level of corruption in religiondom.

"...for that day shall not come,
except there come a falling away first,
and that man of sin be revealed, the son of perdition;
who opposeth and exalteth himself above all
that is called God, or that is worshipped; so that he
as God, sitteth in the temple of God,
shewing himself that he is God.
...that he might be revealed in his time.
For the mystery of iniquity doth already work:"
2 Thessalonians 2:3,4,6,7

"...until the appearing of our Lord Jesus Christ:
Which in his times he shall shew, who is the blessed
And *only potentate,* the king of kings,
and the Lord of Lords;
1 Timothy 6:14,15

A son honoureth his father, and a servant his master:
if then I be a father, where is mine honour?
And if I be a master, where is my fear?
Saith the Lord of hosts unto you, **O priests,**
That despise my name."
Malachi 1:6

175

For both prophet and priest are profane;
yea, in my house have I found their wickedness,
saith the Lord. Wherefore their way shall be unto
them as *slippery ways in the darkness*:
they shall be driven on, and fall theirin:
for I will bring evil upon them, even the year of their
visitation, saith the Lord...
Thus saith the Lord of hosts, hearken not unto the
words of the prophets that prophesy unto you:
they make you vain: they speak a vision of their
own heart, and not out of the mouth of the Lord.
They say...unto every one that walketh after
the imagination of his own heart,
No evil shall come unto you.
For who hath stood in the counsel of the Lord,
and hath perceived and heard his word?
Who hath marked his word, and heard it?
**Behold, a whirlwind of the Lord is gone forth
in fury, even a grievous whirlwind: it shall fall
grievously upon the head of the wicked.**
The anger of the Lord shall not return,
until he have executed,
and till he have performed the thoughts
of his heart:
*in the latter days ye shall consider it
perfectly.*
I have not sent these prophets, yet they ran:
I have not spoken to them, yet they prophesied.
Jeremiah 23:11-12, 16-21

"And now, O ye Priests, this commandment is for you.
If ye will not hear, and if ye will not lay it to heart,

to *give glory unto my name*, saith the Lord of hosts,
I will even send a curse upon you,
and I will curse your blessings:

yea, I have cursed them already,

because ye do not lay it to heart.
Malachi 2:1,2

"Then spake Jesus to the multitude,
and to his disciples, saying,
the **scribes** and the **Pharisees** sit in Moses's seat:
All therefore whatsoever they bid you to observe, that
observe and do; *but [do not do as they do.]*
But all their works they do for to be seen of men...
they love the uppermost rooms at feast,
and the chief seats in the synagogues,
...and to be called of men, Rabbi, Rabbi.
But *be not ye called Rabbi:* for one is your Master,
even Christ; and all ye are brethren.
And call no man your father upon the earth:
for one is your Father, which is in heaven.
Neither be ye called masters: for one is your Master,
even Christ. But *he that is greatest among you
shall be your servant...*
But woe unto you, scribes and Pharisees, hypocrites!
For ye shut up the kingdom of heaven against men:
For ye neither go in yourselves,
neither suffer ye them that are entering in
to go in.
Woe unto you, scribes and Pharisees,
hypocrites!
...therefore ye shall receive the

greater damnation.
Woe unto you, scribes and pharisees, hypocrites!
**For ye compass sea and land to make one
[convert], and when he is made,
ye make him twofold more the child of hell
than yourselves.**
Woe unto you, ye blind guides,
...Ye fools and blind:
...Ye fools and blind: ...
Woe unto you, scribes and Pharisees, hypocrites!...
Ye blind guides,
Woe unto you, scribes and Pharisees, hypocrites!
For ye make clean the outside of
the cup and of the platter,
but within they are full of extortion and excess.
Thou blind Pharisee, *cleanse first*
that which is within the cup
and platter, that the outside of them may be clean.
Woe unto you, scribes and Pharisees, hypocrites!
...(you) are within full of dead men's bones,
and of all uncleanness.
Even so **ye also outwardly appear
righteous unto men,**
but within are full of hypocrisy and iniquity.
Woe unto you, scribes and Pharisees, hypocrites!
...ye be witnesses unto yourselves,
that *ye are the children of them*
which killed the prophets.
Ye serpents, ye generation of vipers,
how can ye escape the damnation of hell?
Wherefore, behold, I send you prophets,
and wise men, and scribes:

and *some of them ye shall kill and crucify;*
and some of them shall ye scourge
in your synagogues,
and persecute them from city to city:
That upon you may come all the
righteous blood shed upon the earth,
from the blood of righteous Abel
unto the blood of Zacharias son of Barachias,
whom ye slew between the temple and the altar.
Verily I say unto you,
All these things shall come upon this generation.
Matthew 23

I AM one with JESUS the MESSIAH
I AM one with Space eternal, everlasting
I AM one with Time eternal, everlasting
I AM one with the HOLY SPIRIT

I AM a smooth, agile, eloquent swimmer
in the sea (reality)

I AM the salt of the earth:
I AM wisdom and understanding

I hold and direct the bridle reality:
I AM one with JESUS The MESSIAH.
I AM one with the HOLY SPIRIT

I achieve in leaps and bounds
I AM power (beauty) in JESUS THE MESSIAH.
I visualize vividly.

Father I AM in thine thoughts, in accord,
in thine thoughts

I AM a successfully influential child of I AM
for ever and ever.

Recite each **SEED** at least 7 times each; over and over every *morning* as you arise, and every *evening* before sleep. Day and night. Night and Day.

Acknowledgements

1. Acknowledging that GOD is the cosmic consciousness that forms the cosmos, and all phenomena in it, the earth, including the observer(s).
2. Giving thanks for the availability of these remarkable pictures of the cosmos through web sites of the public domain, publicly funded NASA, and the Hubble Heritage Team.
3. Also, I give thanks to my wife, my mom and family— for being patient with me; and X, who graciously helped me to format the graphics in my books.

Bibliography

1. The Bible, King James Version.
2. Greene, Brian., *The Fabric of the Cosmos: Space, Time, and the Texture of Reality,* New York, Knopf, 2006
3. Whittle, M., *Cosmology: The History and Nature of Our Universe,* Parts 1-3, The Teaching Company, Chantilly, VA 2008
4. Wolfson, R., *Einstein's Relativity and the Quantum Revolution: Modern Physics for Non-Scientists, 2nd Ed.,* The Teaching Company, Chantilly, VA 2000
5. http://www.infoplease.com/encyclopedia/science/milky-way-size-shape-milky-way.html
6. http://www.nytimes.com/2016/02/12/science/ligo-gravitational-waves-black-holes-einstein.html?_r=0
7. https://en.wikipedia.org/wiki/Earth's_magnetic_field Glatzmaier, Gary A.; Roberts, Paul H. (1995). "A three-dimensional self-consistent computer simulation of a geomagnetic field reversal". Nature 377 (6546): 203–209. Bibcode:1995Natur.377..203G. doi:10.1038/377203a0
8. http://lambda.gsfc.nasa.gov/product/cobe/
9. https://www.physicsforums.com/threads/what-of-an-atom-is-empty.74297/

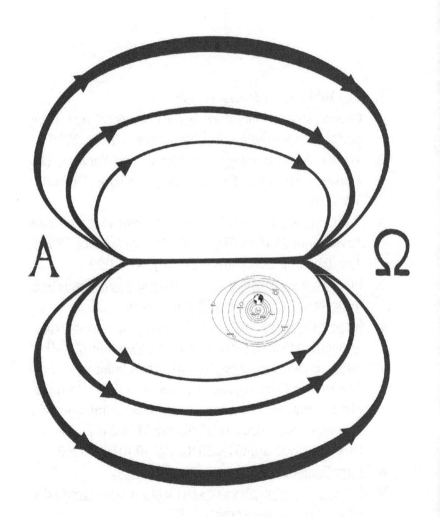

A   Ω